THE ENGLISH SEASON

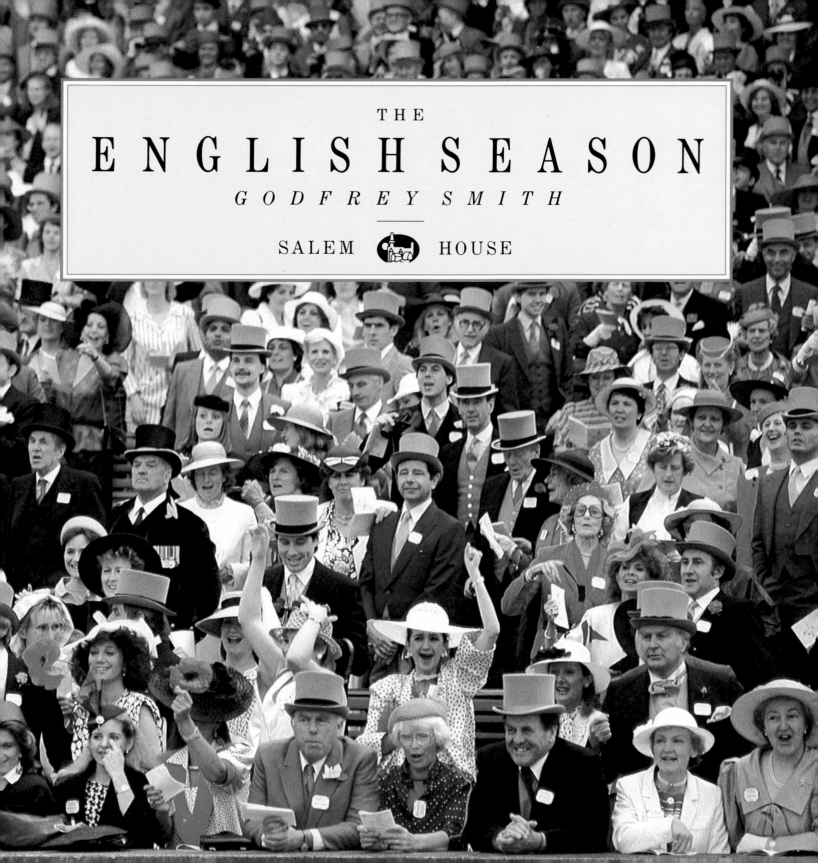

THE
ENGLISH SEASON
GODFREY SMITH

SALEM HOUSE

FOR JOHN AND TORY WITH LOVE

First published in the United States by 1987 by Salem House
Publishers, 462 Boston Street, Topsfield, MA 01983

Designed by John Gorham
Layout by Madelaine Serre
Co-ordinated by Susan Mitchell

Library of Congress Cataloging-in-Publication Data
Smith, Godfrey, 1926–
The English season.
Includes index.
1. England – Social life and customs – 20th century.
2. Upper classes – England. I. Sykes, Homer. II. Title.
DA566.4.S56   1987   942.085   86-31657

ISBN 0-88162-236-2

Printed and bound in Italy by Arnoldo Mondadori

CONTENTS

INTRODUCTION
7

'The English take their pleasures sadly', said the Duc de Sully. Only a Frenchman could say something so demonstrably daft. The fact is that the English have brought to a fine art the trick of extracting the maximum fun from their windswept and rainy little island. No other nation on earth has devised a season with quite so many delights; and contrary to popular opinion some of them are quite cheap and one or two are quite free.

Like many other English institutions, the season tends to change its shape and colour the closer we examine it. The old definition in the OED made perfectly good sense at the time it was written roughly fifty years ago: 'The period of the year during which a particular place is most frequented for business, fashion or amusement; especially the time (now May to July) when the fashionable world is assembled in London.' That was the season in the strict sense to which Anthony Eden referred in his memoir *Another World*: 'In the summer months we would usually take a house in London for the season.' It was the same curious phenomenon to which Virginia Woolf referred in her last novel *The Years*: 'The stream of landaus, victorias and hansom cabs was incessant; for the season was beginning.'

It used to be short. In the reign of Queen Anne, G. M. Trevelyan tells us in his *English Social History*, 'The London season was over by the first week in June when people of fashion dispersed to their country homes or adjourned to Bath. A longer residence in town would have ruined many families who had strained a point to bring their daughters to the London marriage market.' There were those who thought that when the marriage market formally ended, the season would end with it. The presentation of debs at Court ended in 1958 and the last Queen Charlotte's Ball was held in 1977. The prediction could not have been more wrong. The season grows more and more popular each year; and more classless. Paradoxically, it is the participation of the Royal Family in the English season that gives it glamour and focus; yet it is on these festive days that the Royals move most casually among their subjects.

The point is well made by Adam Helliker, editor of *The Debrett Season*, the only systematic attempt to examine the subject in recent years. 'You will see the royal family move with absolute freedom at Badminton,' he writes, 'taking their dogs for walks and chatting to people who share their equine interests. You may see a fleet of tatty Land Rovers which will be carrying various royal personages and a whole host of court officials overflowing from the back, or you may find yourself in the path of a blue or brown Range Rover driven by Prince Charles or Prince Andrew. If Princess Anne is at the wheel the best thing to do is to get out of the way fast because it is a certainty she will be going at speed and will not be prepared to stop for plebs. By contrast, last year Prince Charles took to riding about on one of the Duke of Beaufort's horses and was civil to everyone he met.'

Now all you need to get this remarkable close-up of the royals at play is your entrance money – a mere £6 per car or, say, £1.50 a head. No other social *cachet* is required and nowhere (certainly not in the Soviet Union) do rulers and ruled mingle more freely.

There was a time when any satisfactory definition of the season would have involved the idea that some member of the Royal Family took part. Not any more. In his excellent book, Adam Helliker stretches the season to a full year by including such off-beat diversions as the health farm and the Beaujolais Nouveau race. Neither has any royal patronage and is unlikely to do so – not at any rate until some minor royal takes the cure or helps race the Beaujolais home.

It must also be said of the Debrett year-long cycle – entertaining as it is and most useful to my purpose – that it gives enormous weight to the sporting side of the season. Thus, of the twenty-three main social events it lists, no fewer than nineteen involve some sport or other, five involve horses and another one, dogs. In this book we have leaned a little to the more cerebral side of the season; but the sporting bias remains. This, no doubt, reflects the natural inclinations of the English public, who on the whole would rather see a great horse race than look at a great picture. Obviously, the audiences overlap. You will see some of the same faces at

Glyndebourne as at Ascot; and the Royal Academy will attract some of the young ravers who have been bopping the night away at the Rose Ball. Yet there is no satisfactory definition that precisely encompasses the modern English season.

Certain threads seem still to run through it. Some sort of contest is often involved. With the sporting fixtures this is self-evident; but even at the Chelsea Flower Show there is keen interest in which rose or rhododendron will win the first prize, just as at the Royal Academy Summer Exhibition the interest centres on which pictures have been chosen from the many thousands sent in.

Another curious trait of the English season is that many events in it seem to involve some kind of what one might call fancy dress. It is a peculiarly English proclivity, seen at its wildest at Ascot and Henley (dressing up) and also in a curious way at places like Badminton and Twickenham (dressing down or, at any rate, dressing against the weather).

Similarly it is hard to think of any event in the English season which does not involve lashings of drink: indeed one elegant definition of the English season might be all those events at which the great champagne of Veuve Clicquot is on sale (it will be a long and formidable list).

It also seems to me a characteristic of the season that it will involve celebrities, stars and gossip. Each event tends to have its own stars: Prince Philip at Cowes, the Duchess of Kent at Wimbledon, the Queen at Royal Ascot. Yet though some royal presence set its stamp on any event which was truly part of the old English season, it no longer seems to be a *sine qua non* of the new elements in it. Indeed, like the OED's famous dictum on the English language, the English season nowadays has a well-defined centre but no discernible circumference. In the end, therefore, we have chosen those events which seem to fill out the cycle of the English year most enjoyably.

Finally it must be said that the English season is one of the most instructive and complex ways of looking at the English class system. A radical critic will see it as still encapsulating the old rigid forms; and certainly we can see the outlines of them. However free and easy Badminton is, the Duke of Edinburgh normally drinks in the directors' tent from which the public is banned, while at Henley only the select few get into the stewards' enclosure; but then some system like this will be found in all parts of the civilized world and is dictated by common sense. To the right, however, the season will seem a dramatic proof that all's for the best in the best of all possible worlds. At the Derby for instance, as we shall see, the class structure dissolves in one vast kaleidoscopic blur. The rich arrive in helicopters and the trippers in trains; men wear anything from grey toppers to knotted hankies, women anything from Balenciaga to bikinis. Champagne and Charrington's wash down the lobster and whelks. All human life is there; and what is more, dreamlike in its timelessness.

Thus the English season, shifting at its perimeters, constant at its core, is a hypnotically interesting subject to explore. Let us begin with an archetypally English winter festival.

BOOKS CONSULTED

The Badminton Tradition by B. Campbell, Michael Joseph 1978.
Centenary History of Oxford University Rugby Football Club by R. McWhirter and Sir A. Noble, OURFC 1969.
Centenary History of the Rugby Football Union by U.A. Titley and R. McWhirter Rugby Football Union 1970.
The Chelsea Flower Show by F. and G. Whiten, Elm Tree 1982.
The Debrett Season ed. A. Helliker, Debretts Peerage Limited 1981.
Derby 200 by M. Seth-Smith and R. Mortimer,

Guinness Superlatives 1979.
Derby Day by D. Holloway, Michael Joseph 1975.
The English Game: A Cricket Anthology compiled by G. Brodribb, Hollis and Carter 1948.
English Foxhunting by R. Carr, Weidenfeld and Nicolson 1976.
Henley Royal Regatta by C. Dodd, Stanley Paul 1981.
The History of Croquet by D. Prichard, Cassell 1981.
The Joy of Cricket edited by J. Bright-Holmes, Secker & Warburg 1984.
The Magic Wheel: An Anthology of Fishing in Literature edited by D. Profumo and G. Swift, Picador 1985.

The Oxford and Cambridge Boat Race by C. Dodd, Stanley Paul 1983.
Royal Ascot by D. Laird, Hodder and Stoughton 1976.
The Story of the Guards by J. Paget, Osprey 1976.
This is Wimbledon by A. Little, The All England Lawn Tennis and Croquet Club 1986 (sixth edition).
Epsom Racecourse by D. Hunn, Davis Poynter 1973.
The Eton Book of the River by L.S.R. Byrne and E.L. Churchill, Spottiswoode, Ballantyne 1935.
Glyndebourne by S. Hughes, David and Charles 1981.
The Golden Thread/Foxhunting Today by M. Clayton and John King, Methuen 1984.
The Guards by J. de St. Jorre, Aurum Press 1981.

RUGBY AT TWICKENHAM

JANUARY/FEBRUARY

Twickenham is the opening and closing sally in the year-long feast the English call the season. Despite the rigours of the English winter, it is always a festival marked by high good humour. Rugby football grows more popular each year – there are now seventy-nine countries who play it – and Twickenham tickets get harder to come by. The ground holds 63,000; but the Rugby Union will sell only 61,500 tickets. The reason is quite simple: they cannot detect all the forged tickets that are now an inevitable part of the scene on an international day. One tout was recently found with five hundred on him. As they change hands at £15 each the financial incentive is obvious.

But the ticket touts operate at the modest end of the price scale. Such is the popularity of a day out at Twickers nowadays that two schools whose land adjoins the ground have rented marquee space so that firms can sell a day's outing – champagne, lunch, and a ticket for the game itself – for a handy £200 a time. And sell them out.

Even if you are one of those ordinary fans who buy their tickets through their local clubs your chances of getting what you want diminish yearly; in January 1985 the Rugby Union returned over £700,000 in refunds for tickets they could not supply for the England–Wales game, and they still took £385,000 from those lucky enough to get tickets.

So what is the secret of Twickenham's fascination? First, the game itself is an enthralling one in which movements of great beauty will suddenly flower from what looks like the chaos of maul and ruck.

Everybody will have his most magical try. The most famous ever seen at Twickers is still reckoned to be that scored in 1936 by Alexander Obolensky, a White Russian prince playing for England against the All Blacks. He had learned his rugby at Trent College in America, and that December had already scored a devastating try against the All Blacks in their game against Oxford, where he was then a Brasenose undergraduate. A blond meteor, Obo's main secret was a deceptive change of speed which allowed him to whistle by an opposing defender as if he had gone into overdrive. On 4 January 1936 Obolensky on the England wing had already scored once against the formidable All Blacks, a feat that had a strong influence on the historic second try; for as Obo began his run down the right wing the entire All Black defence raced over to meet him. Sensing that he could catch them all on the wrong foot, Obo suddenly switched his direction in mid-stride, sliced left and scored midway between the left corner flag and the goal-post. He was, alas, destined to die in 1940 in a flying accident while serving with the RAF.

Other connoisseurs will name the try scored by P. B. Jackson against Australia that looked quite impossible; others again the brilliant try, scored, after a run of forty yards and the sweetest dummy, by Dicky Sharp against the Scots; a run so moving that it brought on the birth of a first son for my friend Nick Mason, sports editor of the *London Daily News*, whose wife Jane was at home watching the television broadcast of the game while waiting for her labour to start.

There are other and slightly less spectacular reasons for Twickenham's vast post-war success. Rugby is an evolving game where the laws are still not settled; and sometimes a simple change like that requiring a player to kick for touch from behind his own 22-yard line in order to secure territorial advantage will give the game a whole new dimension of fluidity and visual excitement. Then again there is the fact that every single ticket sold at Twickenham must come from a club (even the £200 ones have started life that way), so that virtually the entire male audience have played the game themselves.

A seasoned Twickers fan will have so many memories that they tend to dissolve into a blur of reminiscence. Still, the game between Oxford and Cambridge on 10 December 1985

*Above: Varsity rugby match, December 1985: one occasion when
all previous form is jettisoned. Oxford won against all the odds.
Opposite: The car park: legendary social focus of the varsity match.*

might well stand for them all. Before that day the two ancient universities had met 103 times. Oxford had won 43 games, Cambridge 47, and 13 had been drawn. Cambridge, with five wins in a row already under their belt, were easy favourites to win a sixth time and so create a new record for the event. The year before they had won a pulverizing game 32-6. It was fourteen years since Cambridge had been outscored in tries, and Oxford had just two tries to show for all their efforts in the last six Twickenham matches. Andy Ripley, the giant former England forward who had captained teams against both university sides, rated Cambridge 4-1 on. Yet none of this matters on the day: all previous form, all known statistics, are thrown out of the window. The Varsity match obeys its own rules and no others.

On a cold, clear, windless day, perfect for rugby football, the unmistakable aroma of embrocation pervaded the air on the west side of the ground, the side where VIPs are seated, memorial tablets stand to rugby internationals lost in two world wars, and the changing-rooms are housed. Tucked away in the official enclosures was the usual line of amber Rolls-Royces, royal blue Daimlers, and black Mercedes-Benzes. Then there were the rank and file punters themselves: the positions of their parties in the park often identified by clusters of balloons tethered to their cars, sometimes white, sometimes in green, silver or blue foil; sometimes a little standard or flag marked the place. The barbaric smell of barbecues mingled with the embrocation. The cigar smoke rose in the still air with the expectations of the massed *aficionados*.

Those expectations were to be most handsomely fulfilled. Oxford had been given a vital talk the previous weekend by Alan Jones, coach to the all-conquering Australian tourists. He told them that if they cut out all fancy play and over-elaborate ploys and concentrated on the traditional rugby skills, they could win. That afternoon Oxford played many levels above their previous best. They did not miss a tackle all day. Their surging back row broke up the endless Cambridge three-quarter movements and they gave the Cambridge stand-off Mark Bailey, an able footballer playing out of position because of previous injuries to his team, a most unhappy afternoon. It was also from a fine spoiling movement that the Oxford back row set up a great try for their No.8, Coll MacDonald. Those four points and three from a penalty goal meant that Oxford turned round at half-time a hardly credible seven points up; and in a pulsating second half, while Cambridge were able to notch up six points from two penalties, they never crossed the Oxford line – though in the last five minutes of nerve-racking, nail-biting play it looked as if they must. But they didn't; and, *pace* Ripley and all the pundits, Oxford won a famous victory.

Philip Toynbee once remarked that a bomb under the West Stand on an international day would end fascism in England for a generation. In sober truth, any lurking fascists are likely to be drowned out by shoals of schoolmasters down from the north, Welsh miners, Scottish pipers, and Frenchmen on a weekend spree from the Dordogne. What you are much more likely to see at Twickers is not the fascist but the publicist. On the day of that Varsity game, for example, I noted, apart from the usual coaches and double-decker buses purveying hospitality to clients, several stylish custom-built vehicles: a very old French charabanc marked Colombes, with a sign saying Dromnibus Gastronomique on its side but in fact hailing from Canterbury; and a scrumptious facsimile of an Edwardian Transit motor car, *circa* 1910, in royal blue, the property of All Seasons Leisure, also from Canterbury. The biggest single hosts at Twickers that day, however, were naturally C. T. Bowring, the giant insurance company, one of whose main reasons for sponsoring the game is the hope of recruiting Oxford men and women.

Nor is your run-of-the-mill punter far behind in the hospitality stakes. There was a time when fans would be content with a chicken sandwich and a bottle of beer; not any more. Nowadays a stroll between the serried ranks of Rovers and Jaguars will reveal an astonishing cornucopia of fare: barbecues grilling anything from bangers and hamburgers to steaks, and Calor gas stoves cooking anything from bacon and eggs to *boeuf bourguignon*. Some people still drink beer, but many more now drink wine and there is plenty of bubbly as well – not to mention the hip flasks which people take into the game for a nip of brandy or whisky between the scrums.

It is an abiding miracle of Twickenham that despite all the booze that goes down – and quite apart from what is consumed

*England beat Wales at Twickenham – always
a triumph, even on home ground.*

in the car park the caterers sell 30,000 pints of beer in the course of the afternoon – there has never yet been any crowd violence at Twickenham. Perhaps this has something to do with the fact that women are as welcome as men and act as a civilizing influence; perhaps it is because the violence is all contained in the field of play and thus sublimated. Or perhaps – most of all – it is because rugby still remains an amateur game. Certainly when the cash comes in at one end of a sport, the fun seems to go out at the other.

How long this will remain so is anyone's guess; but the pressures against amateurism are immense. It is hard to convince a young player that he should display his skills for nothing when such vast sums now flow into the sport from advertising and sponsorship. There is also the vexed question of the debentures.

When the Rugby Union decided to build an enormous new South Stand so that the field would be surrounded on all four sides by stands they had to raise £3.5 million to do it. They therefore issued five thousand debentures worth £350 each. All a debenture can do for you is give you the option to buy an international seat for ten years. It was hoped that clubs would buy them up; but they failed to do so, and they were therefore put on the open market. They were snapped up by big business, and cannot now be had for love or money. With them go no fewer than 812 car park tickets in the West Stand. Since players and officials must have car space too, that exhausts the thousand spaces there. The charming East Car Park, with its famous oak tree as landmark, disappeared when the RFU built their headquarters block up there; so now only the North Car Park remains with its thousand places for the ordinary rugger fans. In practice each rugger club receives one car ticket and, hardly surprisingly, there is a brisk trade in them and forgeries have begun to appear here too.

'So anyone going to Twickenham should be warned never to buy a ticket from a tout. There is a little ticket office outside the main entrance, open on international days, where returned tickets are sold. When 61,000 people are involved there will always be some who simply cannot get there after all; so you need not be left out on the great day. To get the best out of Twickenham you must get your car there by 11 a.m. (the gates

are open at 8.30 a.m.) and because of the huge traffic jam afterwards you are unlikely to get away much before 6 p.m. – a perfect excuse for a second picnic and a chance to dissect the nuances of the game.

Twickenham is probably the friendliest of all the great festivals in the English season and arguably the booziest. It is also a vivid example of how the English triumphantly overcome the hazards of their appalling winter; for the famous floating festival and the Twickenham picnic goes on whatever the weather sends. So wrap up warm and don't forget your hip flask.

How to get in

For the home internationals, as we have seen, you really need to join a club and apply through them, or importune a friend who belongs to a club. Many join several clubs to be sure of international tickets. An old Welsh international joined a Scottish borders club because, as he pointed out, the demand up there for England-Wales tickets was muted. On the morning of the big game, the ticket box mentioned by Air Commodore Weighill is open at no 3 entrance from noon for the sale of returned tickets, but be early; there can be up to 500 in the queue. If money is no object, you can get a ticket from Payne and Gunter, the caterers at Twickers, which provides morning coffee, lunch, tea, a bar with unlimited drinks till an hour and a half after the game, and your ticket. Cost: £75 for the Oxford-Cambridge game; £199 for an international. They also have a very limited number of car park tickets to go with these packages: first come, first served. For the university game, though there is still a fair crowd, there is never a sell-out, and you can always buy your ticket at the gate, or get one at the RFU ticket office in advance. From the 1987-8 season the RFU are also running a credit card sales telephone number: (01) 891-2333. Payne and Gunter will be happy to send you a dossier of all their services at (01) 741-2245. Even at their substantial prices, it's as well to be in touch with them in the April before the rugby season opens.

How to get there

In A.G. Macdonnell's magnificent novel England Their England, *chapter 7 is devoted to arguably the funniest account of a village cricket match ever written. Much less well known is his account of a visit to the Oxford-Cambridge rugby game at Twickenham in chapter 11. Donald, the innocent young Scottish hero, travels on the train from Waterloo to Twickenham with thousands of other rugger fanatics who are still not sure of the result when they get back again at 6.25 pm. This is still the simplest way to go, as well as the most fun, and BR lay on dozens of extra trains. It's a 20-minute journey, then a 7-minute walk. Or if Waterloo is not a convenient starting place, take the tube to Richmond and one stop on the train from there to Twickenham. There are buses, but they are best avoided on international days and are in any case likely to be diverted. Cars should head down the A316 from Hammersmith on the 10-mile journey; but we can't emphasise enough – start early. If you have no car park ticket reserved for Twickers itself, make for the Harlequins ground next door where you can buy one provided you're in time on the day. Not such fun, but a quicker getaway.*

THE BOAT RACE

MARCH

Of all the sporting events in the English season the Oxford and Cambridge Boat Race is perhaps the most bizarre. Less than one per cent of the population has attended either university, and of that one per cent probably only a tenth have ever pulled an oar. Nevertheless, and despite the press of other attractions, the duel over 4 miles 374 yards between Putney and Mortlake has a weird and enduring compulsion.

As Harold Macmillan, recalling his childhood, told the 199 Blues and their guests assembled at the Savoy to celebrate the 150th race in 1979, it 'meant something quite extraordinary to London. And everyone, the whole of London, the costermongers, the drivers of four wheelers, those delicious hansom cabs – the gondolas of London, as Disraeli called them – everyone cared about the Boat Race. All wore the colours, light blue or dark blue. In the household everyone, the housemaid, the butler … there were great divisions. My father was at Cambridge, so as a child we were Cambridge. Nannie was violently for Oxford. And on the day, on that great day, the whole of London, people in offices, streets and homes, cared only for this great event.'

The crowds may not now be quite so big as they were in Victorian times, when there were fairs all along the towpath and the race was an excuse for a family day out. Yet still each pub along the Thames has its knot of spectators; still several thousand wait for the finish at Mortlake, where there is still a small fair and flea market; still eleven million watch the race on television in this country; 150 million throughout the world.

Paradoxically, though only one crew can win and that one is often evident after the first few minutes' rowing, the race continues to provide its crop of dramas, comedies and tragedies. Both crews have known the ignominious experience of having their boats sink under them. Cambridge sank in 1859,

1912 and 1978; Oxford beached in 1912 and sank in 1925 and 1951. In 1984 the Cambridge cox steered his mighty men flat out into a moored barge under Putney Bridge, thus wrecking the boat and causing the race to be postponed and rowed on a Sunday for the first time. The introduction of women coxes has also provided gratifying media coverage for Ladbrokes, the betting giant that financed the race from 1977 until 1986 (Burroughs Gin has just taken over). Susan Brown was the first woman to cox a winning crew when she steered Oxford to victory in 1982, and Carole Burton took an impeccable line when she steered Cambridge to their first victory for ten years in 1986.

From the point of view of the men in the Blue boats themselves, the exploit must sometimes appear to verge on the lunatic. In America oarsmen are usually not chosen until they reach university, when young men with the right height and physique are selected and intensively trained from scratch. In England most – though not all – of the oarsmen will have rowed at school. For many, therefore, the idea of rowing in the Boat Race will have been haunting their imaginations for anything up to seven years.

The trials are held each November and from January, when the crew is chosen, till Easter, when the race takes place, the young men undergo a horrendous training schedule. They must be prepared to devote five hours of their day to running, gymnastics and of course the rowing itself. Few rules are necessary: the young men are quite motivated enough without that. They don't even need to worry about diet; they can burn up to 6-7,000 calories every day. If you can imagine lifting fifty-six pounds from your feet to your neck thirty-four times a minute for eighteen minutes, you will have some idea of the gargantuan physical challenge they face in the race. Obviously they will take very little alcohol, though on the night before the

*Above: Some of the Cambridge crew test their muscles on dry land,
carrying the boat away from the water.
Opposite: Prince Edward: Cambridge man and prize-giver on the
day Cambridge came back to win in 1986.*

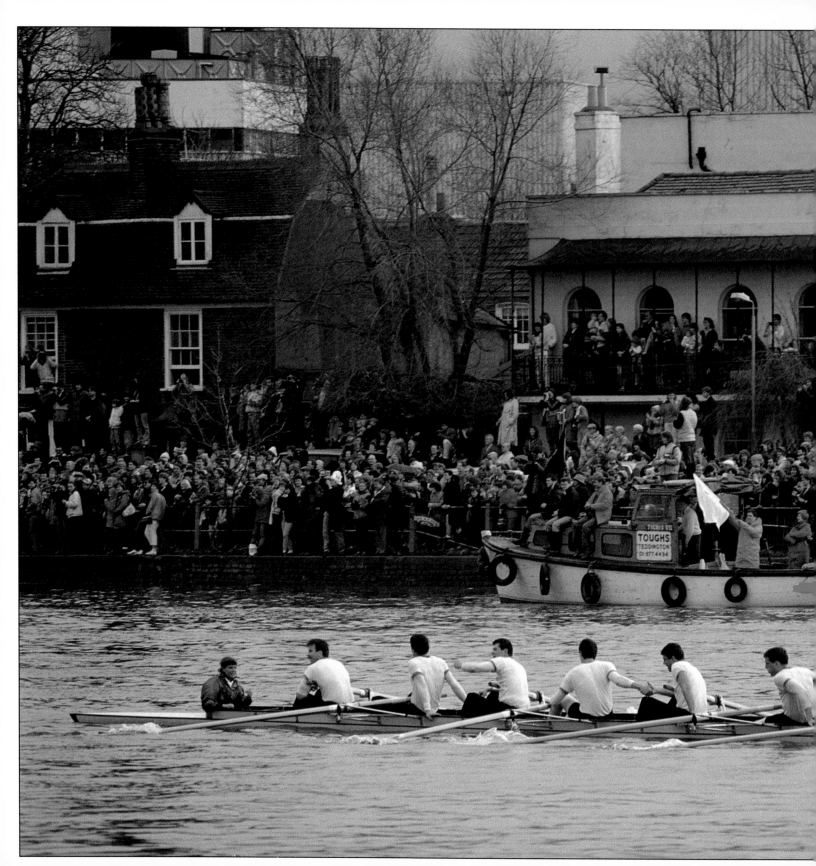

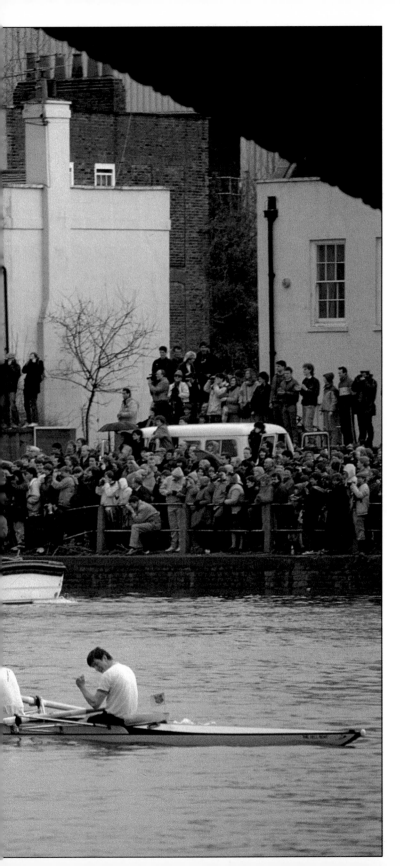

race it is the pleasant Oxford custom to sit around drinking port and discussing the strategy and tactics for the next day.

Certain schools have predominated over the 157 years since the first race was rowed, and Eton has supplied no fewer than a third of all rowing Blues. However, nowadays the young man in a Blue boat is more likely to have a first degree in microphysics or metallurgy behind him from an American or Australian university. He is also likely to stand six foot three inches and weigh a little under fourteen stone.

Whereas there once may have been some truth in the old joke that Africa at the height of the British Raj was a country of blacks ruled by Blues, nowadays the *cachet* is much less. Indeed, in applying to many Oxbridge colleges you are advised not to mention your rowing ambitions; tutors frown on the long hours away from books or laboratories. So what precisely is the fascination of this obscure and exigient sport?

For the participants perhaps the elemental pleasure in being tuned to a peak of physical fitness they will never attain again; and then the indefinable pleasure of rowing in a frail shell-like craft that sings through the water with seven other men in perfect harmony. And, besides, there is always the uncertainty of how it will turn out. In the 1985 Boat Race, for example, the issue was in doubt until the twelfth minute.

Psychology is a prime concern in honing a boat race crew. Thus, Dan Topolski, the guru behind Oxford's ten-year winning streak that ended in 1986, said after the 1985 race that four of his eight men had been scared stiff, while six had rowed before in other losing crews. His task had been to make each one believe he was a winner.

So how should this incomparably odd English sporting event best be seen? One good way is to buy a ticket on one of the flotilla of launches that follows the race. In 1986, for example, I was on board the Port of London Authority's spanking launch *Royal Nore* with, among others, the proud parents of the giant American, James Pew, rowing at No.6 in the winning Cambridge boat. We went up to Hammersmith before the race, turned round, and tied up at the pier so that we were facing back down towards Putney and had a grandstand prospect of the long curve in the river from the mile post past the Harrods Depository up to Chiswick Eyot. So we had a

Cambridge crew – and, as always, the winners look much less tired than their vanquished opponents.

head-on view of Cambridge majestically leading Oxford by a good three lengths, then the umpire's launch and the armada of little boats carrying press, radio, and television crews and sundry fans. The armada swept right by us; we cast off, circled, and joined in line abreast to follow the remaining three miles with the others. We also had on board a small television set, so that we could watch every nuance, every comment, every interview, and every shot of the race when we felt like it.

Alternatively, you can go to one of the boathouses at Putney, watch all the preparations and the tossing of the coin for Middlesex or Surrey station, have a drink at the Star and Garter, or the Duke's Head with its panoramic view of the start, then watch on television from there. Even better is to get yourself invited to one of the many private parties that take place in houses along the river; the author A. P. Herbert, a Thames *aficionado*, gave a famous one at his towpath house for many years, and so next door, rather improbably, did Stephen Spender the poet. But if you don't have the entrée to a private party, you can join the fun at one of the riverside pubs along the path of the race; the Blue Anchor just under Hammersmith Bridge; the Rutland right next door; or the ancient Dove, favoured watering-hole of celebrities from Ernest Hemingway to Graham Greene. To finish the day in style, you must grab a taxi and make for the Ibis and Quintin boathouses at Mortlake where the crews come ashore for their Veuve Clicquot champagne and their trophies; a ceremony undertaken after the 1986 race with some charm by the Cambridge undergraduate Prince Edward when his university so dramatically and resoundingly broke Oxford's ten-year run of victories by that seven-length win.

And then there are the celebrations that night. In keeping with the rigorous and slightly eccentric traditions of the race, the two crews dine separately afterwards, though they do meet and mingle later in the evening at the Boat Race Ball in the Savoy Hotel. Tickets for this can be bought at a price, and will enable you to mix freely with the young giants who have just participated in this most arcane of English sports.

How to get in

The race can be watched by anyone from the Thames river bank, but naturally the best places for spectators (the start and the finish) are snapped up early on the Saturday morning. The two boats are followed by a number of launches and steamers, on which clubs such as the Victoria League take a number of seats for members keen to see the action from the water. The organizer of the Boat Race, Mr Duncan Clegg (tel:01 588 2721), can advise on ways to buy places on such craft.

How to get there

The race is run from Putney to Mortlake in south-west London. Travelling by car can be annoying as traffic is heavy and parking is difficult. The alternatives are taxi, bus, British Rail train to Putney or Mortlake or Underground (to Putney Bridge station by the District Line). The steamers and launches leave from Putney Pier.

The Grand National is the greatest steeplechase in the world and also has some claim to be the greatest soap opera. It nearly always provides romance, drama, comedy and, sometimes, tragedy. It is unique in a vast assortment of ways. It is the only venue in England which is in use for only one meeting a year. It is the most democratic of institutions: anybody can go and anyone can place a bet. Some £50,000,000 is wagered on it in sums ranging from 10p to £30,000. It is a terrifying test of horse and rider; but the very nature of the fences can alone bring the best out of a really great horse like Red Rum, the only horse to win Aintree three times and be second there twice.

It is a race that is full of political and business dramas. The Topham family owned the course for nearly a hundred years; but in 1964 the last Topham who owned it, Mirabel, began to claim, with some justice, that it made no economic sense to use the course for three days a year, and she therefore proposed to sell it. For many of the following twenty years the great race was continuously off and on, but happily Seagrams, the giant drink conglomerate, recently took a ten-year option on the race which still has seven to go. Although, with the advent of television, Aintree no longer attracts the astonishing half a million who went just after the war, it will usually pull in 50,000 people to enjoy one of the great bonanzas of the English sporting year.

They will be able to enjoy not simply great steeplechasing but a host of sideshows. They will put away 100 cases of gin, 70,000 cups of tea, 200 lb of smoked salmon, 100 turkeys, and 500 cases of champagne. They will be wearing no fewer than 50 different types of badge and will pay anything from £2 for the Aintree Enclosure to £25 for the chance to see the race (or at least some of it – no vantage point allows you to see it all) from the County Stand and Paddock. It is one of the easiest places to get to – the M62, which connects to all the main motorways in England, will take you to within a mile of the course.

Real connoisseurs like to stay the night before at a pub or hotel (Southport is now considered a better bet than Liverpool) so that they can be on hand at 7 a.m. when the horses go for their last canter and there is a final chance to judge them.

It is a race that is full of extraordinary records. But it is not a race for favourites. In this century only five outright favourites have won it and five joint favourites. On the other hand there have been four 100-1 winners, the most recent being Foinavon in 1967, survivor of the havoc caused by loose horses at the twenty-third fence. It is a good race for amateurs: altogether gentlemen riders have triumphed in thirty-eight Nationals.

It is a race that has produced one best-selling writer in the shape of Dick Francis, the champion jockey who will always be remembered for the moment when the Queen Mother's horse, Devon Loch, suddenly collapsed under him when he looked a clear winner. It is a race that has produced heroes like Bob Champion, who came back after recovering from one of the worst forms of cancer to win in 1981, a day on which there was hardly a dry eye in the vast concourse. It is a race which is now seen by courtesy of BBC TV by an awesome five million viewers. It takes more than two hundred BBC staff, twenty-two cameras, twenty miles of cable, three directors and two weeks of on-site preparation to get the coverage right. Only a royal wedding or funeral would command greater outside resources. It is not so much a horse race; more a slice of life.

How best to see it is a moot point. Some people like to take a radio and picnic and go out to a favourite jump; others prefer the razzmatazz of the paddocks. The stands were allowed to deteriorate badly during twenty years of indecision, but a lot of work has been done to restore them and all this work is beginning to pay off. There is now a swish restaurant, a host of chalets and marquee, where big business can entertain its guests in style, and a new stand which has been dreadfully dubbed 'the raised viewing facility'; but wherever you go to watch you are bound to see some drama.

A single white tape stretches across the width of the course at the start. Ahead of the runners lie four and a half miles and thirty of the world's toughest fences. Despite the senior steward's pre-race warning to take the first fence easily, far too many horses go at it headlong, and this is where many make their first mistake. Then comes Becher's Brook, immortalized by Captain Becher, who took a header there the first time the race was run (remarking later that water without brandy tasted even worse than he imagined), and which still

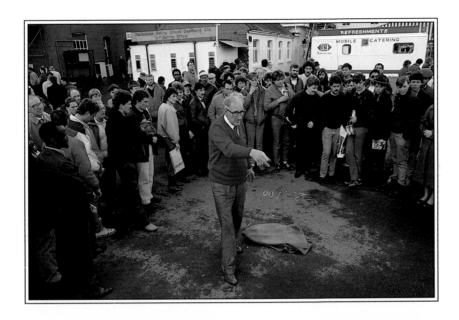

Above top: An Aintree tipster offers his thoughts for the day – at a price.
Above bottom: Grand National owners come in all shapes and sizes.

proves a daunting test of horse and rider. Then comes the Canal Turn – not so much a great problem to jump but a hard one to negotiate because of the ninety-degree turn after landing.

Next comes Valentines Brook, smaller of the two Brook fences, but not to be lightly dismissed; and then several fences later comes the mighty Chair with its 6ft wide ditch just before the 5ft 2in high fence, probably the most formidable of all the Grand National fences. Then, as if that were not enough, there is the water jump; with its 2ft 6in high fence and 12ft span of water, before the moment comes to take the circuit a second time.

In 1985 the race lived up to its dramatic traditions when it was won by a horse that was widely held to be a bit of a rogue and which was only entered by Anne, Duchess of Westminster, to placate its importunate jockey, Hywel Davies. Not a single sporting tipster in the national press gave him a chance and the only time he was mentioned on the morning of the race was in an interview given by the housewives' favourite, Richard Dunwoody, a jockey who knew the horse because it came from the same stable as his own. Last Suspect – a fitting name for such an unexpected winner – came home at 12-1, leaving the bookies with most of the £50,000,000 in their pockets, and proving once again the unpredictable magic of the great steeplechase.

In 1986 *The Times*, which had said of Last Suspect the year before 'can be safely crossed off your list', sportingly gave a whole page to Hywel Davies's own dramatic account of how he had done it. 'You know immediately whether the horse has gone over the top, whether the build-up has sent him over and he's bottled out on you and lost confidence, or whether he's revving and going for it. ... I knew that Last Suspect was in that sort of mood as we approached the first. When he caught sight of it his ears were pricked, and he was looking for it, feeling that he wanted to jump it ...

'Becher's is phenomenal. From the take-off side it looks a perfectly normal fence. Horses that have never jumped it before don't know there's a big drop the other side and they jump it just like any other fence. Half-way over they realize and they just kind of freeze, they stop breathing, their mouths open. They must die the death, because there's no ground there, it's just gone. But old Sus was great over it, like an old gentleman should be. Preservation was foremost in his mind. He just glided down and landed softly ... I gave him a real big kick on the fence before the Chair. I wanted him to fly over so that he'd do the same over the next. The Chair is a daunting fence, but he met it spot on ... he absolutely flew.

'Becher's second time round ... I thought "Hey, we've got a great chance of getting round, unless something dreadful happens".... He was fine until he came to the third last, when he dropped his hind legs on the fence. But that was my fault. I tried to shorten him, and I should have allowed him to run and jump the fence. As we landed I was saying to myself, "Oh you idiot." I thought I'd finished his chances.

'I came into the straight and suddenly realized there were only two fences to jump. I looked to see how many horses were in front of me. I saw the two leaders going away, Corbière and Mr Snugfit, and I looked to my left and Greasepaint was there, but under pressure, and I thought, "I'm going to be third, third in the Grand National. Fantastic."

'He flew the last fence and landed running, and then I suddenly realized, "My God I could be second," because I could see Corbière was tiring. His head was on one side.... He agreed to pass Corbière and when we got to the Elbow I put my stick in my right hand and I saw Mr Snugfit about three lengths ahead. So I really belted him one, the hardest I'd hit him at any stage. And he just went.... He said to himself, "All right, I've been thinking of that, but I'll do it now." And voom, he flew.

'And then as I passed Mr Snugfit it hit me. "I've won the National." And then I realized how exhausted I was.'

In the 1986 National Hywel Davies was again among the forty starters on Last Suspect; but this year the old gentleman had had enough, and did not want to know about the race; he was pulled up at the eighteenth fence. Yet the inevitable soap opera story-line continued to unfold. For Richard Dunwoody, at twenty-two the youngest rider in the race and the same baby-faced housewives' favourite who had been alone in tipping Last Suspect in 1985 (a year when he himself fell), was back to win a cool and brilliant race on West Tip – a horse which by rights should have been put down four years earlier. He had a dreadful

Previous page and above: The hazard of hooves at the great
Aintree jumps.

Richard Dunwoody, the housewives' favourite, who came home
against the odds in the 1986 Grand National.

accident with a lorry, which left a gaping hole in his side that needed eighty stitches to repair.

The 1986 race was full, too, of the customary heartaches. You could hear the great groan from the massed fans in the stands when the much fancied and heavily backed Door Latch fell at the first. All the favourite, Mr Snugfit, could do for his owner, millionaire commodity broker Terry Ramsden, was a modest fourth place. This meant that Mr Ramsden, instead of being yet another million better off, as he would have been had Mr Snugfit won, was still some £150,000 richer from his accumulator betting. The 66-1 outsider Young Driver was the only horse in the end to give West Tip any real trouble; old stager Classified was third; the great 1983 winner, Corbière, fell; Essex, the totally unknown outsider from Czechoslovakia, carrying top weight, went well but pulled up at the fifteenth. Yet not a single jockey or horse was seriously hurt on that horrendous ride.

A rich feast, then, for the Aintree enthusiast. Grand National Day is best begun early; certainly at 10 a.m. there are still no crowds and parking is easy. The rise of the ubiquitous forger means security is tight: at the entrance an attendant will mark the little white circle on your badge with a special pencil to make sure it comes up pink; if it doesn't it's a forgery. Whenever you leave the course your wrist gets a green stamp that doesn't wash off for a day. The main entrance is pretty with its green and white awnings, and its noticeboards directing you to some of the course's principal attractions: the private rooms, the parade ring, the bookies and banks, the Café Continental and the Sky Restaurant. To the left of the entrance is a row of shops selling everything from trilbys and sweaters to sporting books and binoculars. If you are a keen student of form you will want to buy the Timeform race card at £3.60, thus furnishing yourself with the minutest details of every runner's past history and track record. If you are a keen student of racing history, you will want to stop at the little white stand in which all the trophies that will be raced for are on display: a fine sculptured bronze of a jumping horse for the winner of the National; silver plate and cut glass for lesser races; magnums of champagne galore. However, you will comfort yourself with the fact that the real guarantee of the race's integrity lies in the whopping prize money – £42,691 for the winner of the National alone.

Near the shops stands the charming little weighing room and unsaddling enclosure with its ornate green ironwork pillars, white wooden roof, and baskets of spring flowers. Here sits the BBC anchorman Desmond Lynam, who in 1986 had a dual role, for he is the proud proprietor of a horse called Another Duke, a 200-1 outsider which nevertheless carried the money of various sentimentalists and royalists anticipating Prince Andrew's summer nuptials. Lynam said that should he win, all his usual BBC training and decorum would go out of the window. No such luck; Another Duke was destined to fall at the ninth.

On the wall of the weighing room there is a plaque to the legendary Red Rum with a poem inscribed on it; not great poetry perhaps, but written *con amore:* 'Some horses come, some horses go, whose names will last for years/And one of these is with us now whose feat brought floods of tears.' Yet never believe Red Rum is only remembered in a stone verse; the lovely bay horse was there in person to parade before the stands, a flower worn jauntily in his ear, to take another ovation from the crowds before the races. No race-goer is more sentimental than your average Aintree punter.

There is still time for a saunter along the course to inspect those awesome jumps at first hand; some women have recklessly worn high heels, which are fine if you propose to stay in a private box all day, but hell out there in the mud. At the fearsome Chair a local fan sums up: 'A horse needs heart to jump that bugger.' A woman takes a fir branch out of it as a souvenir. Now the bookies are putting up their stands and raising their multi-coloured umbrellas. The stalls in the middle of the course are already doing a brisk trade in hot dogs, burgers, bacon sandwiches and coffee. A few seasoned drinkers are already supping beer. There are precious few chairs at Aintree, and it's a good idea to bring a shooting stick; you will be standing, if you haven't booked a seat, for four or five hours.

Now it's time to make your way back to the County Stand, another charming, Edwardian-style building with white balustrades, rows of hanging baskets full of spring flowers, and, on the lawn in front, a great bed of daffodils and hyacinths.

Underneath the stand is a row of Tote offices, so that you can place your bets without ever going out; though the bookies who line the County Stand rails will also be happy to oblige if you prefer their odds. The tic-tac men with their day-glo green and white gloves are now busy signalling the changing prices; but now perhaps it's time to go into the Lawn Bar under the stand where you can drink anything from Guinness to Clicquot and eat anything from lobster and prawns to smoked salmon and roast beef baps.

The best view of the racing is undoubtedly from the roof of the County Stand, but remember, if it's wet the only way to keep dry is by reserving a seat in the terrace below. Wherever you watch from in the County Stand, though, you will have in front of you the giant screen on which each horse and rider will be meticulously reviewed in turn: its form, its current price, and the colours its jockey will wear. If the screen has become more real for you than reality, you can watch the whole race on it. And then, in case you still don't have enough data to decide, the horses will make a slow, stately parade right in front of you Before they go down to the start. Aintree has done all it can to make you happy; the rest now is down to those forty great horses and their intrepid riders.

How to get in

The County Stand is steeped in tradition and full of racing memorabilia, including the stuffed head of The Wild Man of Borneo, the winning horse in 1895, and the colours carried successfully by Lottery's rider in 1839. The cost in 1986 for this stand was £28, giving spectators a fine choice of dining and tea facilities, and a selection of champagne or wine bars, not to mention the chance to rub shoulders with the racing hierarchy. Either side of this stand are Tattersalls and the Silver Ring, neither of which boast enough catering facilities for comfort, and which cost £12 and £7 respectively. The Western Enclosure and the 'Cabbage Patch' cost £2.50 each, while the country viewing areas represent good value at £1.

How to get there

Aintree is five miles from the centre of Liverpool. To get there by road, the M6 leads on to the M62 which in turn leads on to the M57, taking visitors to within a mile of the course. There is an excellent train service from London via Birmingham, and coaches run from all major towns.

BADMINTON

APRIL

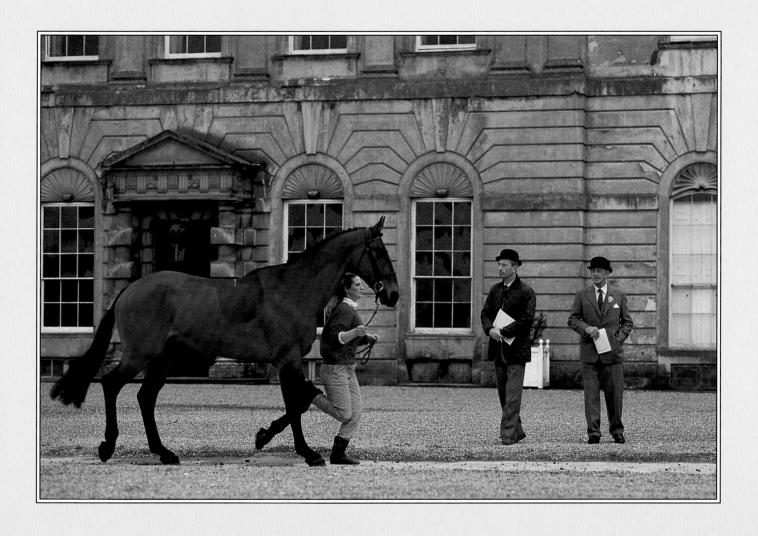

If you were anxious to study the widest possible cross-section of English society, your best bet might well be to head for Badminton. For at this relatively new event (held here since 1949) you will see how the Royal Family at the same time put their stamp on the event and melt into it with total informality. A quarter of a million people go each year now on cross-country day alone; 300,000 over the four days; and no other event in the sporting calendar attracts so many English people except perhaps the Derby.

Although the horsey world is there in force, you don't have to be horsey to enjoy Badminton. Probably if you are not horsey the best sport is to saunter up and down the 250 trade stands that make up a canvas village during Badminton, purveying every possible horsey want and a good many more. Here you can buy top boots and saddles, Huskys and sheepskins, horse-boxes and shooting-sticks. Here you can buy pictures of horses and even hand-coloured verse pictures about them ('there are verses galore/about old hunts of yore' and so on). You can insure yourself against a nasty fall at Stable, Stud & Farm or even put your child down for a good school at the Independent Schools Information Service. Should you have young children in tow the Norland Nannies will be happy to look after them for up to two hours - the best possible advertisement for their young ladies who go out to staff the nurseries in every part of the globe. While it is not quite true that you can buy a tiara at Badminton, you can certainly pick up a handy rope of pearls for £1,850 at Garrards, the Crown Jewellers, or a picnic basket at Aspreys which would not have disgraced Hudson, the imperturbable butler in the television series *Upstairs, Downstairs,* for a mere £265.

You can eat fish and chips or cockles and mussels, hot dogs or pizzas, lobsters or smoked salmon. You can drink beer – but only Whitbreads, for they sponsor this vast event handsomely – or champagne. Indeed, every taste is catered for at Badminton, and the gradations in dress are infinitely subtle, reflecting differences in style more than in class or income.

The classic symbol of Badminton is the green welly – an object of some derision for the non-horsey world; but in fact when it has been raining or snowing the course soon turns into a quagmire and green wellies prove essential. Otherwise anything goes; but the Puffa or sleeveless quilted jacket and the waxed overcoat have become *de rigeur.*

All you need to get into Badminton is £6 for your car (£12 on Saturday for the cross-country). If you want to watch the dressage and jumping in secluded comfort you can join the British Horse Society on the day by paying £5. This admits you to their comfortable enclosure, making up one side of the ring with its own bar and chairs and tables for tea outside. It is also possible, by paying a nominal sum, to join the Beaufort Hunt Club, which entitles you to drink in their tent. Otherwise the only other worthwhile expenditure is a stand ticket to watch the show-jumping properly on Sunday and get a good view of the Royals. This will cost you a fairly modest £5.50 each.

Badminton started when the grand old 10th Duke of Beaufort went to watch the first Olympic Games after the war. All the equestrian events were at Aldershot, and the Duke walked the cross-country course with his old friend Colonel Trevor Horne from Luckington. It was during the picnic lunch which followed that he first mentioned the idea of holding a similar event in his park at Badminton. That first year there were a mere 6,000 people; but the interest and participation of the Royals very quickly put it on the map. Princess Anne has been European Champion and her husband, Captain Mark Phillips, has won Badminton four times.

The fascination of Badminton is its curious mixture of the

*Above: Princess Anne where she is most at home: in the
dressage section of Badminton.
Opposite: Green wellies, Barbour jackets, and Aspreys – a typical
Badminton day.*

patrician and plebeian. Thus, with a largesse which belongs to a different age, the Duke stables all the horses competing. No other event in the world houses all the competing horses in permanent stables. Badminton feeds them free of charge. It also pays for the grooms to be fed in the servants' hall, surrounded by scores of antlers and the trophies of former hunting trips, as well as by a vast number of copper pots and pans. The total prize money is now £25,000 for the top twelve places, a mere trifle compared with some sports; but then horse trials are still an amateur sport and the prestige of carrying off one of the trophies counts quite as much as the cash.

Yes; but what exactly are all these riders *doing?* They are taking part in a contest called competitive eventing. Originally a sport confined almost entirely to the military, and stemming from the horse trials conducted in the Army, it has been popular on the Continent for many years; but was hardly known in Britain till after the Second World War. Many people who came to the first contest at Badminton quite seriously thought they were going to see a game played with racquets and a shuttlecock.

In fact, what they saw was an equestrian version of the modern pentathlon; an all-round test of horsemanship which calls on almost every activity of which a horse is capable. Just as the Fourth of June at Eton seldom occurs on that day, so the Badminton three-day event covers four days because the first discipline, dressage, takes two days. The object of dressage is the harmonious development of the physique and agility of the horse. To achieve perfect understanding with its rider, the horse must be calm, supple and keen. Of course the repetition of the same baffling manoeuvres by some seventy competitors may pall for the uninitiated; but even here the sight of so many beautifully groomed animals and so many elegant riders is both pleasing and restful. Still, things do speed up a bit after this.

Next comes the speed and endurance phase. This is cross-country day, when some of the world's leading riders tackle thirty-four awe-inspiring jumps. They have names like Huntsman's Grave, Vicar's Choice, and Lamb's Creep, and include obstacles like hedges, ditches, fallen trees and a jump over a jetty into a real lake, then a leap out of the lake over a

Spray, tents, water, crowds – all the necessary props for the scene at Badminton.

boathouse. More than one member of the Royal Family has taken a right royal purler in the cross-country, which may do something to account for its vast box-office draw. Then on the last day comes show-jumping – far more accessible to the man in the street because it has become a vastly popular sport in its own right. A complex points system decides who the overall winners are.

Even the layman can see the drama which can be generated by a close-fought finish; as in the 1985 event, when the local heroine, Virginia Leng (née Holgate), who lives only two miles from Badminton, just pipped the New Zealand Olympic gold medal winner, Mark Todd, who would have won had he not displaced a pole in the very last fence of the triple jump. In 1986, in a morass of mud left by the incessant rain, Ian Stark provided drama of a different sort by slithering to a popular win on Sir Wattie. 'He jumped his heart out for me,' Stark said afterwards. He had successfully held off the challenge of twenty-one-year-old Rachel Hunt on Piglet II, who complained when she entered the arena that the rain was coming down so hard she couldn't see the fences. Stark, the first Scot to win Badminton since Anneli Drummond-Hay in 1962, spent eight years as a civil servant before becoming a surprise choice for the Los Angeles Olympics. There he knocked down one fence at Santa Anita, but helped Britain win her silver medal and, as Frank Keating remarked in *The Guardian*, 'was a conscientious life and soul of a happy team, always ready in the stables to bring up the rear with good heart, saddle-soap, the bucket and spade'.

Eventing is in international terms Britain's most successful sport of all; we have won more Olympic, world and European championship medals in it than anybody else. It is a sport which has been called the ultimate test of both horse and rider. Col. Frank Weldon, who designs the cross-country course at Badminton, has gone on record about his intentions: 'I aim to frighten the wits out of the riders but never to hurt the horses on the day.' It is this fine blend of hazard for humans and regard for the horses which gives Badminton its edge and brings riders from all over the world. Any foreign tourist wanting to understand England would do well to make it his first stop.

How to get in

Entrance charges for cars and all occupants is £13 for the highly popular cross-country day and £6 for the dressage and show-jumping days. A season ticket, which gives entrance to all four days, costs £22, and many who have these tickets arrive early to compete with each other for the front row position which gives the best view of a number of fences on cross-country day. Some even have their breakfast behind their cars. A grandstand seat is necessary to watch either the dressage or show-jumping heats and these cost between £3 and £7. For £7.50 you can book a Sunday seat in Row C to watch the show-jumping which will give you a wonderful seat overlooking the Royal Box.

How to get there

Badminton is in Avon in south-west England. It is 106 miles from London and by car you can get there by going straight down the M4, leaving the motorway at Junction 18. Then take the A46 to the B4040 and watch for signs. The journey from London will take a good two hours and on cross-country day an early start really is necessary to avoid the queues of cars waiting to get into Badminton Park. Trains go from Paddington Station to Swindon but from then on it has to be by bus.

THE ROYAL ACADEMY SUMMER EXHIBITION

MAY

The Royal Academy has now been displaying British art for 217 years. It is hard to realize now that in the eighteenth century there was no way to see what painters were doing, because there were no public art galleries. You might just be privileged enough to get into a royal or private collection; otherwise you just had to go on the Grand Tour. So in 1768 a group of artists asked King George III to give his blessing to an academy that would both teach painting and exhibit it.

The first show, in 1769, contained only 136 pictures. It took place in a hired room in Pall Mall. Later the show moved to the splendid rooms at the top of the new Somerset House - such a high climb that Queen Charlotte had to recuperate on each floor before going up to the next, and Dr Johnson said it was a major test of endurance. After its first hundred years, the Academy moved to Burlington House in 1869 and in its first year there had to make its choice from 4,500 works submitted. In 1986 there were 12,500 works by hopeful artists and only 1,593 were chosen.

The Academy has gone through some turbulent ups and downs. It has seen the advent of abstract art and it has gone through a trough of critical contempt. Yet now it is abstract art which suffers from critical neglect; there is some in the show, but figurative art is back in fashion. Not all of it, however, is conservative or respectful. Hit of the 1985 show was undoubtedly Ruskin Spear's saucy picture of a leering Margaret Thatcher.

The snag for potential buyers is that there are now so many 'Friends of the RA' who, for £18 a year, are allowed to go to one of the private views, that there is a scrum and the ominous little red dots indicating pictures which have been sold cluster all around you as you walk in.

Spare a thought, though, for the artists, because this is their show too. The cardinal charm of the Royal Academy Summer Exhibition is that anybody can have a go, and from any part of the world. The fact that your chances of getting a picture hung are slim (as we have seen, roughly one in ten) and that you have to pay a fee (£7.50 per work) to be considered discourages most overseas artists (though paintings do arrive from the Middle East and Italy). Yet you never know your luck. Sir Hugh Casson, who was President of the Royal Academy from 1976 to 1984, and is a distinguished watercolour painter as well as a world-famous architect, remembers in one of his early years there a boy of eleven having his picture accepted. 'My own experience,' he says, 'is that it's very hard to resist naïve pictures. They have great charm, these old ladies who paint people in supermarkets. The lack of self-consciousness makes up for the lack of technique.' Another category which is hard to turn down is what he calls 'the very careful *trompe-l'oeil* or those Victorian dolls. You can't say you're turning them down just because you're tired of them. The *skill* is the same year after year.'

The judges, though, change all the time: 'If seven people don't like cats one year they'll get in next.' Only two judges have to like a picture for it to survive the first viewing; that does not get it in; merely gives it a question mark. The pictures go by the judges so quickly that it's hard to think that they can possibly take them in; but most selectors have been experienced teachers all their lives and many still are; it does not take them more than a few seconds to make up their minds. Certainly the students who act as porters have usually made their own minds up about the wares they are carrying. 'It's not hard to spot what I call the Hyde Park railings pictures,' says Sir Hugh.

There are evident inequities. If you have a room which can hold a hundred pictures, and you have two hundred to choose from, the question of how they relate to each other must play a part in deciding what's in, what's out; in the end there may be

Above: The Royal Academy – centre of Establishment art.
Opposite: The moment of truth – will that picture make it?

room for only one more picture eighteen inches by four feet with not too much blue in it; and that is the one that will prevail even if another picture has more merit. Nor are artists immune to what they must hang next to; Turner would come in and make adjustments, perhaps painting in a woman in a scarlet cloak, if he thought he was being upstaged by the painting next door. Artists still add last-minute touches, but more nowadays in a spirit of desperation than out of any real sense of emulation.

There are of course inequities too on the buyer's side; and emulation as well. This is the only show where you can see two hundred people running up the stairs as the first private view opens – with cheques for pictures they will not even bother to look at; they will have been tipped off about them beforehand. In the 1984 show, 1,166 pictures were sold on the first day – one every 24.7 seconds. Their average price was £225. Then there is the vexed question of the Annual Dinner on the eve of the opening. Suppose a cabinet minister or a bishop, trooping round the show when dinner is over, sees a painting that takes his fancy – is he to be denied? Not usually; and it has been known for one of the well-paid electricians with the BBC crews there to televize the speeches to get out his cheque book and buy that night too. Or what if some iconoclastic millionaire with a sense of fun and a fat bank balance decides to buy two hundred pictures at the private view, as Victor Lowndes once did? To be fair, he thought that the prices were too cheap, left the paintings on the walls and got people to bid higher for them, donating the difference to charity. It worked. But I can remember the sense of anti-climax, as one of the run-of-the-mill punters, on coming in on one of the members' days and seeing that great rash of red dots facing me.

For the artist this sort of largesse is double-edged. On the one hand, it is marvellous to see his pictures sold. On the other, he wants his work to be loved for itself; he does not want it to be part of some enormous job-lot. He likes to feel an empathy between painter and buyer; and I can testify to the private courtesy that impels a painter to sit down and write to the stranger who has bought his picture, thanking him for doing so. For the painter, this is the ultimate reward; just as to be rejected is his ultimate dread. The great English original Stanley Spencer once remarked that you never forget anything nasty said about your work; in his case, a notice in the *Colchester Gazette* ('we have no use for Mr Spencer's bluff allegories') still rankled. And the President of the Academy will receive some thirty tear-spotted letters from rejected painters which he will try to answer personally. The pain of rejection is not only emotional but may also be material; if you are one of those painters who do watercolours of dirty seas the Royal Academy show may be your only market-place; you may well sell out all your paintings there and live off the proceeds for the whole of the next year.

The price of his pictures is something which is entirely in the discretion of the artist. If he goes to a London gallery, he will be charged forty or fifty per cent commission. The Academy used to charge no commission at all; but, to Sir Hugh Casson's sorrow, when he took over it became necessary to start levying a fee; the Summer Exhibition was costing the Academy £70,000 or £80,000 a year and the bottom of the barrel was getting perilously close. So the Academy began to charge a commission; at first it was fifteen per cent, more recently twenty-five, and they hope never to go higher. The levy seems to be added on to the picture's price but not to hinder sales; they have never been higher than they were last year.

For someone like Sidney Hutchison, who apart from service in the 1939-45 war has spent all his 57 years of working life at the Academy, first as a junior clerk, then as librarian, then as secretary, and finally as honorary archivist, certain externals have changed; but not the fundamentals. The Academy has held an exhibition every single summer since its first in 1769. Before the war, the private view day was always on the Friday before the first Monday in May and was widely held to be the start of the old London season (as we have seen, it has now expanded until it covers most of the year). When Hutchison began work in 1929, although people still spoke in whispers, great ladies like Lady Cunard held court on private view day, perched on a convenient settee with her entourage around her. The Lord Mayor still came in his coach; a discreet Academy employee stood by with dustpan and brush to clear up when the horse had gone.

In those far-off days no woman was invited to an Academy

Visitors arriving in the courtyard of Burlington House

dinner, even though there were distinguished women academicians like Dame Laura Knight; they were first invited as recently as 1967. Before the war it was Hutchison's task to write out by hand each card for the private view: His Grace the Duke of this, the Most Honourable the Marquess of that. Recently at the Academy dinner he sat next to a young man who wore neither the white tie prescribed nor the black tie now accepted in lieu, but an ornate and attractive cravat. His card was inscribed with neither lord nor the hon. nor plain mister; but simply with the gnomic word Sting. He turned out to be the leader of a pop group and proved highly agreeable company; the world has moved on in the 57 years since Hutchison started.

He has seen nine presidents. Each has contributed something to the Academy; even the famously reactionary Sir Alfred Munnings, painter of horses, who launched a celebrated attack on Matisse and his school at the Academy dinner of 1949. It was Munnings who hit on the idea that Sir Winston Churchill, who for many years had the satisfaction of seeing his work, submitted under a pseudonym, chosen for the Summer Exhibition, should be created honorary academician extraordinary. Munnings did not, however, live long enough to see the pop star, Tommy Steele, have one of his pictures chosen for the summer show too.

Even if it's no longer true, as it was in the Victorian era, that everyone is expected to go to church on Sunday and the RA once a year, it is still a high point in the social calendar. You may see an American film star adding to his Beverly Hills collection; or one of the more civilized cabinet ministers; or you may see the veteran jazz man Humphrey Lyttelton touring the galleries. But it's still possible with great care and cunning to buy a small print or etching in the low hundreds.

But the modern Academy contains an extraordinary range of talents – all the way from painters Peter Blake and John Bratby to sculptors Elisabeth Frink and Ralph Brown. And though when Sir Hugh Casson retired as President people felt it would never be the same again, his successor, Roger de Grey, has stamped his own style on this curious English festival of art. He is a sixty-eight-year-old Etonian who has been Principal of the City and Guilds of London Art School since 1973 and who runs the Academy from a modest table in an office on the first floor with his secretary at a desk beside him. One of the drawbacks of the presidency is that it necessarily involves a lot of desk work and keeps a painter from his canvas; the President nevertheless reserves Fridays, Saturdays and Sundays for his own work: 'I can't live without painting.'

He does not believe the RA show is any longer a very grand society event: 'It can't be, with 35,000 Friends of the Royal Academy and three private view days.' Although sales totalled £922,177 in 1986 it's still difficult to sell pictures worth over £20,000 and some sculptures. And he emphasizes the difficulty for the private buyer when the big battalions are in the market-place: 'I've bought heaps of works at the summer show – for organizations like hospitals and art galleries.' He is adamant that the Academy is no longer the home of orthodoxy: 'You *can't* have an orthodoxy in the twentieth century.'

How to get in
To become a Friend of the Academy you pay £22.50 a year. There is a concession for teachers, museum staff, etc., who pay £17; for OAPs and those between sixteen and twenty-five it is £15. Visitors living at least seventy-five miles outside London can become Country Friends for £15 a year. Otherwise you pay at the door for an ordinary ticket to the exhibition after the private view day. It opens in late May/early June and runs until mid-August.

How to get there
The Royal Academy is in Piccadilly next to the Burlington Arcade and almost opposite Fortnum and Mason. When the Summer Show is on a special flag is flown over the entrance (a different one each year, designed by an Academician). It is a short walk from either Piccadilly Circus or Green Park tube station and many buses pass the door – so will taxis for a little more money.

THE CHELSEA FLOWER SHOW

MAY

Exasperating and enchanting by turns, ludicrously amateur in some ways and in others relentlessly professional, breathtakingly beautiful in some places and downright ugly in others, the Chelsea Flower Show is a handy microcosm of modern England. It is also a true mirror of the changing face of society; the days when country landowners walked round on Members' Day with their head gardeners, discussing new plants and ordering trees and shrubs for the next autumn or winter, are gone (though a *frisson* of the old order was felt as late as 1947 when a well-dressed woman approached a young assistant on the Clarence Elliott stand, looked at the *Gentiana acaulis* and said briskly, 'I'll have five thousand of those. Send them round to my gardener. Lady Northcliffe. Good morning.')

The Royal Horticultural Society has held its annual show in the grounds of the Royal Hospital at Chelsea since 1913. Before that, as Faith and Geoff Whiten relate in their lively book *The Chelsea Flower Show,* it had been for twenty-five years at the Embankment Gardens of the Benchers of the Inner Temple near Charing Cross; but by the turn of the century relations between the Templers and the RHS had turned sour. The eminent lawyers did not like the noise, the mud, and the cooking smells that emanated from the show, and in 1913 the Chelsea site was booked for a rent of £500. It had three times the space of the Temple Gardens, and twice as many exhibitors applied. Luncheon was served (impossible in the Temple), and City men could still get there directly on the Tube by taking the District Line from Mansion House to Sloane Square. The 1914 show was an even bigger success, but the First World War effectively halted its onward march (though small shows were held in 1915 and 1916). It began again in 1919, on a slightly subdued scale, and has not really looked back since, though the RHS was again on war duty from 1939 to 1945, informing and educating on fruit and vegetable growing and co-operating with the Ministry of Information on lectures and films.

It is a show that has always enjoyed royal patronage; the Prince Consort was President of the fledgling society until his untimely death in 1862, and the royal connection continues with the annual visit by the Queen on the first Monday evening while the judges are still making up their minds about the awards. Not every Royal, however, shares the Queen's predilection. Once,

when the redoubtable Miss Beatrix Havergal offered the old Duke of Gloucester one of her renowned strawberries, he declined. 'Spoils the port' was his verdict. But he was an exception.

It's almost too popular. There was a time when you could go on Members' Day and have a chance to look at the gorgeous profusion of flowers in comfort. But since you can join the Royal Horticultural Society outside the show by simply putting down your £14 that is now as much a scrum as any other day. When the doors open at 8 a.m. there are already several thousand people waiting. It would probably be better for the show to move over the river to Battersea Park, where there would be much more room; and the RHS is indeed considering this possibility now.

The great point of Chelsea is that while you can send for catalogues, here you can see the best that British nurseries can grow in one place. All the famous growers are there, but there are also slightly more offbeat firms who specialize in old roses – some of which, they believe, were grown here even before Roman times.

For the gardener, obviously, there is no other way to see quite such a treasury of beautiful flowers under one vast marquee (which itself covers three and a half acres and takes two dozen men more than two weeks to put up). Everyone has a favourite flower, but in 1985 the ramrod-straight delphiniums, ranging from the palest white to the deepest blue, took some beating. So did the foaming sea of rhododendrons, ranging from blinding white through pink to rose and cyclamen, and through lilac and lavender to the profoundest purple. In 1986 it was the turn of the pink roses: all the way from Pheasant, a deep rose pink shown by Mattocks, through Leaping Salmon from Rearsby Roses, to Sexy Rexy from Sealand Nurseries – soft, pink, and resistant to rain and sun.

So there is exquisite beauty to be seen – but also some rather square and dreary landscapes and gardens. Although you will see some elegantly dressed people in the huge crowds, frankly sensible tweeds and flat shoes are more suitable for the aching miles you have to walk. The brass band lends a homely rural note and the Chelsea Pensioners provide the most colourful sideshow. The catering is adequate and the coffee

Previous page and above: The Chelsea Flower Show: excellence,
beauty and skill – an art at which the British excel.
Overleaf: A Chelsea pensioner gets among the prize winners.

45

strong – but avoid the Danish pastries, which can be as heavy as Copenhagen cannonballs.

Chelsea is an oddity in the English season because it is the one event in the long cycle of the English year where the Queen is a keen patron but does not mix with other fans. She will have gone, after her private tour, long before *hoi polloi* arrive. The social hub of Chelsea is the President's Tea Party on Tuesday afternoon; a mixed bag of ambassadors and mayors, together with a few genuine gardeners, some 370 in all, each one individually vetted by banker Robin Herbert, President of the RHS, and received by him personally after being announced at the door. Here you will see a sprinkling of the old aristos mingle with showbiz people who are genuinely interested in gardening, like Anna Ford and Penelope Keith, or who are having a rose named after them, like Nana Mouskouri, Susan Hampshire, Cleo Laine, and Esther Rantzen's baby Emily.

The purest showbiz, though, comes in the last couple of hours before the show closes on Friday. Every exhibitor has to get a certificate from the RHS to confirm that he has cleared his space to the satisfaction of the Society – who are in turn responsible to the Hospital. So now is the time for the bargain hunters on the prowl for exhibitors selling their wares off cheaply. As the bell goes at five o'clock, bedlam sets in as buyers scramble for plants. They say you don't need to ask the way back to Sloane Square station on the last night; you just follow the trail of delphinium petals. The great marquee is empty at last, the tired flower fanatics trudge away, the gardens deserted. It is time to start planning next year's show.

How to get in

To join the Royal Horticultural Society and thus get a Private View ticket for the show it is now no longer even necessary to apply for membership by writing in advance of the show dates. Anyone who wishes to join can enrol at special kiosks at the entrances off Royal Hospital Road and on the Embankment on Private View Day, when the show is open from 8 a.m. to 8 p.m. A subscription of £24 gains entrance to all the Society's meetings and shows and includes two tickets for the Private View. Although the Private View tickets are transferable they may be used only once. A subscription of £14 buys most of the members' privileges but only one Private View ticket. For both classes of membership there is also an enrolment fee of £5.

How to get there

Taking a car is not very wise as there is simply nowhere to park and the police are quick to remove illegally parked vehicles. Taking a taxi is really the best way of getting there, but the Underground is the next best choice. Take the Circle or District Line to Sloane Square and then walk. It is best for visitors travelling by car, taxi or coach to alight at the Embankment entrance.

TROUT FISHING

MAY

'As soon as you think of fishing you think of things that don't belong to the modern world,' wrote George Orwell. 'The very idea of sitting all day under a willow tree beside a quiet pool – and being able to find a quiet pool to sit beside – belongs to the time before the war, before the radio, before aeroplanes.' The philosopher J. W. Dunne saw an even more profound reason for its fascination. Unlike any other sport, your opponent was none other than nature herself, 'wayward, cheating, laughing, alluring, infinitely diversified, entrancingly mutable'. And the Poet Laureate, Ted Hughes, himself a keen fisherman, has pinpointed what we can only call its mystical thrall: 'You are aware, in a horizonless and slightly mesmerized way, like listening to the double bass in orchestral music, of the fish below there in the dark.' We know that the ancient Greeks fished (Homer has lively fishing passages in both the *Iliad* and the *Odyssey)*; but the Chinese may well have known the art long before that. Here, though, we shall be considering only fishing in England; and even within that wide ambit (the island race can boast three million anglers) only the most aristocratic of all its forms: dry- fly fishing on the Hampshire Test, that king of all trout rivers (though the devotees of the neighbouring Itchen might dispute that).

John Birth, who was shortly to celebrate his fifty-third birthday the day we first met on a lovely stretch of the Test, was also about to celebrate his half century as a fisherman. He lives in Northumberland, and begins fishing for salmon on the Tweed when the pheasant shooting ends on 1 February. He stays on the Tweed till mid-April, then comes down to the Test, where he stays with his guests in a rambling, comfortable 300-year-old A-frame cottage full of fishing pictures and memorabilia. Here he entertains the company to the unending fascination of his reminiscences about the art of angling, excellent cooking, plenty of drink, and the best trout fishing in the world. That day he had three French fishermen staying, two with their wives. They come to England because, John says, fishing in their own country was basically ruined by the French Revolution: 'They messed it up. Everybody could shoot and fish, which ruined it for everybody. You can't kill and murder everything. You must take a little and not too often. The idea is not to catch monsters but to keep the river going.

*Above: The sort of tackle a Test fisherman takes
with him to capture the speckled brown trout.
Previous page: John Birth, fisherman, at work on an
enchanted stretch of the Test.*

I had a chap here fishing the other day who caught a five-pound trout with black spots the size of your thumbnail. He said I hope you won't mind but I put it back in the river. He was right. You look at it, you say, how beautiful, and then you say bye bye. I'll swear they wink at you. If you do knock them on the head they look at you most reproachfully.'

This policy of careful conservation has paid rich dividends on the Test. 'The French come here in great humility and admiration.' Like the Australians, Americans, Germans and Italians who make their way to this fisherman's nirvana every spring, they are prepared to pay handsomely for the privilege of staying in a cottage close to the banks of the Test and the chance to fish both banks along two miles at no more than four rods a time.

Basically, there are two broad kinds of fishing in fresh water: coarse fishing, usually with live bait such as worm or maggot, for such homely English fish as roach, perch, pike, chub and tench; and fly fishing, with the artificial lure of cunningly wrought imitation insects which will appeal to the majestic *salmonidae* family of fish – salmon, trout and grayling. Here, however, another great division opens up: between the salmon fisherman and the trout fisherman.

The trout is hatched, lives, and dies in fresh water. If he is offered something that looks to him like food, he will take it because he is either hungry – very hungry at the end of a lean winter – or not hungry at all but just plain greedy if he has gorged himself on dead mayfly in the spring. But as far as catching trout is concerned, food is the name of the game. The salmon, on the other hand, hatches out in fresh water, lives most of his adult life in the sea, and returns to fresh water averaging seven or eight pounds to spawn. Nature sees to it that the salmon comes home from the richly stocked sea so well fed that he can and does live on his accumulated fat. He does not need to eat at all. If he takes a fly, it will be out of curiosity, not necessity.

Which provides the greater sport – salmon or trout? For John Birth, there can only be one answer: 'All the finest fishermen I've known have graduated from salmon to trout.' Yet even among the trout fraternity, there is another great debate: dry fly or wet fly?

Dry-fly fishing owes its modern formulation to the work of several great pioneering fishermen of whom F.M. Halford was the most influential. He laid down a dry-fly code which stated that artificial flies should always be imitations of natural flies in their winged stages and should always be fished floating on the surface – hence, dry fly. Then along came another great fisherman called G.E.M. Skues, who concentrated on trout feeding below the surface, who will not rise to a floating fly, and found they will sometimes take it if it becomes waterlogged and sinks. He published his early conclusions in 1910 in *Minor Tactics of the Chalk Stream*. Thus was another major schism created in the closed, obsessive world of the fly fisherman.

Some thought his new method would not work; others thought it would work all too well; above all, his critics thought his ideas unsporting. 'The fuss and bother!' commented John Birth. 'The flies on this river spend up to two years as larvae, then have a metamorphosis, live for two or three days, then die; hence the lovely word ephemera. You have tens of thousands of them in the air. Then Skues said, to hell with this, I'm going to make imitations of larvae underneath the water. The dry-fly fisherman and the nymph fisherman became first and second class citizens. In 1938 the row became so acrimonious that they decided to have a grand debate in London. Poor old Skues was there. They battled away for a whole evening. These were not cloth-cap types – QCs and the like. It's still going on – the nymph versus the dry fly. I myself prefer dry fly. I love it – probably because I'm not skilful enough to use the nymph. But, by God, if I were to throw a nymph on this river at this time of the year!' Some things, in this private, other-worldly code, are simply not done. John picked up one of his favourite rods, and one of his favourite mayflies, and we went fishing.

The cottage stands by an enchanted stretch of the Test with no special name, though some have suggested it should be called Bacchus pool, after John's dog. Bacchus loves to fish, even more than to go shooting. He will go into the water to fetch what John has caught and bring it ashore in his mouth without hurting it. He sat patiently while John surveyed the prospect before us. 'The wagtails are hawking. If you see swallows or wagtails swooping down low, it means that fly is hatching from the water. Wagtails are not so adept as swallows but they flit and flutter over the weeds to catch and they're lovely.' We stood side by side, drinking in the pastoral scene. 'If I stand here with my hands in my pockets there's a good reason for it. You just watch. It's the great contemplative art. Dry-fly fishing is sixty per cent watching, twenty per cent tactics, ten per cent making your attack, ten per cent playing and hopefully landing your fish. Now today the water's a tiny bit coloured, there's been so much rain. Eight days ago we had a terrible thunderstorm. The river went dead. The fish could feel the barometric pressure drop and just sank to the bottom of the river.' By now John was casting, each time landing his fly some twenty-five yards out into the stream. 'Everything has to go upstream,' he explained. 'This is one of the big debates. Other people say you can fish downstream for a fish which is impossible to catch by casting upstream because of an obstruction to your cast, but we never do it on this part.'

He cast again, caught his line in a tree behind him, but quickly cleared it. 'You need as much space behind you as in front. Casting's like learning to swim or ride a bike – you finally get the knack.' A ring of water clearly showed where our quarry lay. 'There's one there. He might be what we call a "oncer". You want to find a fish that's rising steadily and confidently.' He continued to cast slowly, patiently, every minute or so. Another circle in the water. 'Did you see that? He didn't rise to it, but he boiled, as we call it. I haven't frightened him but he's just not bothering to join in the fun and games.' He decided to change his fly to the locally made sedge, which is exactly the same as the fly which caught the five-pound brown trout in one of the cases in the cottage dated 28 May 1926. 'We'll give it a go; it's not quite the time of day for it but I've a funny feeling it'll do the job.' He greased it well to make it float and cast again. Suddenly the line went taut. 'By Jove,' John ejaculated. 'We've got him!'

The trout swam valiantly back and forth. 'It's a beauty,' John judged. 'A little under two pounds I'd say. We'll let him sort himself out. You can lose them very easily. I've lost more fish under this bridge than I've got pounds in the bank.' This time, though, there was no escape for the trout. Bacchus paddled in and brought him ashore. John inspected him lovingly,

took the hook out of his mouth, and put him back in the water. The trout disappeared downstream under the bridge to collect his thoughts. 'He'll be all right,' John decided.

It was time for lunch. The Frenchmen came in with tales of mixed fortunes on the river. There was an excellent celery soup, a chicken, a bottle of 1962 Château l'Arrosée, some good cheeses, strawberries and thick cream. John talked to his French guests in the sort of homely French Winston Churchill might have employed, but inter-laced with plenty of technical fishing French. 'I like the French,' he said. 'You might think it a worry to have a crowd of strangers on your hands. But it works. I love people. I love whipping a team of strangers together. Of course you have to have certain rules. Someone tied up a monstrous fly the other day and I said, "If you fish with that in my river it'll be for the first and last time."'

In the *Magic Wheel: An Anthology of Fishing in Literature*, the editors, David Profumo and Graham Swift, try to define the secret of fishing's evident fascination. 'Water,' they claim 'is all. More than anything, it is that glinting, tantalizing horizontal veil, the surface of water, dividing so absolutely one realm from another, which gives angling its mystery, its magic, its endless speculation.' To get a glimpse of that magic, try going fishing with John Birth.

Where
Many fishermen consider the southern English chalkstreams the finest of all British rivers for trout. It used to be hard to find fishing on such rivers at short notice, but day tickets for some stretches are now available as well as season 'rods'. Advertisements for day and season fishing often appear the winter before in the magazine Trout and Salmon *(address: Bretton Court, Bretton, Peterborough, Cambridgeshire, tel. 0733 26466).*

When
Many chalkstreams do not open for trout fishing until 1 May, but precise dates of seasons for different catchment areas may be found in Where to Fish, *a 500-page guide produced by* The Field *magazine (address: Carmelite House, Carmelite Street, London EC4, tel. 01 353 6000). The Regional Water Authorities of England and Wales determine the local opening and closing dates for salmon and trout fishing on every river within their jurisdiction. Rod licences for trout are necessary and are issued by the Water Authorities.*

Note
Anybody who thinks he would enjoy trout fishing with John Birth can contact him care of the celebrated fisherman's shop, Farlow and Co., 5 Pall Mall, London, SW1, tel: 01 839 2423.

THE ROSE BALL

MAY

The last presentation of débutantes at Court took place in 1958; a demise regretted by very few. The last Queen Charlotte's Ball, the social face, as it were, of the royal charade, was in 1977; and when that went many voices were raised to claim that the old London season was over. Insofar as it stood for a marriage market into which the nubile daughters of the upper crust were launched, that is no doubt so; and good riddance too. Still, the old forms and shibboleths are not so lightly overthrown; and vestiges of the traditional season can still be detected in the generalized rave-up which has taken its place. One such vestige is the Rose Ball, a whopping dance in aid of Alexandra Rose Day, so named after Queen Alexandra, the consort of Edward VII.

Nowadays the present Princess Alexandra has taken over as president of Rose Day, 17 June, and the profits from the Rose Ball which is its social end are disseminated to a wide range of good causes: from the Friends of the National Heart Hospital to the Royal National Mission to Deep Sea Fishermen and from the British Polio Fellowship to the Jewish Blind Society. All sorts of nobs lend their names to the shenanigans. Patrons include the celebrated Margaret, Duchess of Argyll and the Italian Ambassador; the 120-strong committee includes people like Mrs Winston Churchill and Lady Duncan Sandys; and there is also a junior committee with many a gilded name on board: Tiarks and Warburg for starters.

All this elaborate façade is really the excuse for an upmarket shindig. The deb and the deb's delight may have handed in their dinner plates; but there is no shortage of goose-pimply Sloanes and chinless Young Fogeys prepared to whoop it up in Park Lane till the small hours. New names and new money may take the place of the old; but the revels go on. As Cyril Connolly famously remarked of Proust's visit to the opera in *A la Recherche du Temps Perdu*: the faces may change; but the box is still there.

It was assuredly still there on Thursday 15 May 1986 when some thousand people thronged the Grosvenor House Hotel's banqueting room, the biggest in Europe, to do no more than enjoy themselves as much as their tickets at £35 a head would allow. Though there was a sprinkling of older people, the predominant note was youth; phalanxes of Hooray Henries,

many in dinner jackets, but some thirty per cent in the white ties and tails that are increasingly fashionable among the Thatcherite young. The girls looked as they always did: pretty and expectant in décolleté ball gowns, gossiping and intriguing as they have at such balls these hundreds of years now. It was about nine when the first tables began to fill up for Trust House Forte's good old standard nosh-up: *crêpes aux fruits de mer* followed by *suprême de volaille* and then *cerises noirs jubilee*. At 10.50 p.m. Nat Temple took the floor with his No. 1 Dance Band and the party was under way.

Nat, who has dominated the dance band business in England for four decades now with good reason, launched the revels with Glenn Miller's 'American Patrol', and in a trice the couples were on the floor in a racy quickstep. That great trumpet solo, or at any rate a lively pastiche of it, rang out over the bopping young rich just as it had first done in the Second World War. Then Nat reached even further back, feasting them on 'Alexander's Ragtime Band' and Ory's 'Creole Trombone' with its joyous oompahing solo. Then came a set of moderate rock numbers, and the inevitable Sinatra songs ('New York, New York'). Then some more rock and 'Begin the Beguine'. By 11.30 the tables had broken up into informal, gossiping small groups. Peter Townend, the *Tatler*'s man for all seasons, stood chatting over a drink, his thinning hair falling in an informal lick over his forehead. At our table, presided over with gentle charm by Lady Grade, joint deputy ball chairman, there was no great surprise when her husband, the fabled showbiz tycoon Lord (formerly Lew) Grade, after moodily puffing his inevitable cigar for a bit, made his excuses and left the ball early. It was not his kind of scene.

Whose was it, though? The cameras of London Weekend Television were there to record the action for a four-part series on wealth. The American television company NBC were there too for a cognate purpose: a portrait of the Sloane Ranger, who was indubitably out in force this night. 'Stupendous Car Raffle' cried the glossy ball programme. 'The Exclusive Lancia Y10 Rose, very generously personalized and donated by H.R. Owen.' And there indeed was the Lancia itself, at the top of the steps leading down to the dancing, all glittering in the smoke-filled air. Tickets were a tenner apiece; and the Lancia was won

Above: Dancing flags as the evening lengthens.
Previous pages: The Rose Ball – and Thatcherite England at play.

by a young woman called Miss Sophia Ashton-Bostock, whose father, David Ashton-Bostock, interior designer, was joint chairman of the ball. She ran up to get her prize, a kiss and a huge bouquet. Then, if you had the right number on your programme, you could win what the programme called 'A Superb Diamond Ring', donated by Aspreys and valued at £2,250. A young man in braces and blue cummerbund won that. But these glossy symbols of conspicuous consumption were mere pace-setters. In the Grand £5 Note draw you could win a week's holiday at Barbados; or another for two in Naples with air fares paid. As a result of all this high splurging, between £40,000 and £50,000 would be handed over to the Rose Day funds, and from there to over four hundred charities. Nat Temple launched into his second set with an appropriate number: 'When You're Smiling'.

Then it was time for rock; and now some four or five girls at our table whose partners were otherwise engaged took the floor together, gyrating and undulating in a kind of hypnotic trance where, though each girl performed alone, each was linked to the other in an unlegislated, invisible bond of sound and movement: there are no wallflowers at a modern ball.

Midnight: and by now the mood was entirely relaxed. The light show sprayed cones of blue and orange and red on to the pulsating ravers; girls by now were sitting on chaps' knees. In the men's room the white-tied scions of moneyed families left their 20p pieces in the plate for the attendant; one doesn't get rich by throwing it around. Margaret, Duchess of Argyll, heroine of one of the steamiest of all post-war divorce cases, took the floor with stately and well-groomed dignity; she looked as if butter wouldn't melt in her mouth.

It was not much of a night, though, for the gossip columnists. Phoebe Manners, a niece of the Duke of Rutland, was there; and so was Frances Roche, a cousin of Princess Diana. That was about it. A woman who had been going for thirty-five years said this was one of the quietest yet. Perhaps, she thought, the fact that while once parents paid for their tickets, now the young were expected to fend for themselves,

may have taken the edge off the high jinks. In previous years there had been so many tickets sold that they had put tables up in the balcony; not this year. Nor did the rave-up continue in the park as dawn came up, as had been the fashion in previous years. Perhaps this was because some young groups were seen leaving soon after midnight for other discos which would carry them through to dawn; the Rose Ball ends decorously at 2 a.m. Perhaps as well the competition from other balls is beginning to tell: the Caledonian Ball, for example, goes on till 5 a.m. and costs a mere £25 a head.

Yet there are two ways of looking at it. Peter Townend, the man who for many a long year has compiled the list of suitable young men for debs' mums (and if you're not on his list, you're out as far as the private cocktail circuit is concerned) told me he had enjoyed the Rose Ball much more this year simply because it had been more quiet. When the ball was over-subscribed, he pointed out, you could hardly get to the loo for the crush. And because they had now stopped selling after-dinner tickets, you no longer had young people turning up drunk and stealing Lady Grade's roses. The Caledonian Ball was all very well; but it was an after-dinner affair that began at 9.45 and only provided a breakfast at midnight - if you could get it in the scrum caused by 1,300 people. 'Young people need a good dinner first, so that they don't get drunk, and their parents around to keep order,' he affirmed. 'Otherwise it can become like an East End riot.' And he should know.

How to get in
Write to Mrs Laurie Weston, Alexandra Rose Day, 1 Castelnau, Barnes, London, SW13 9RP or telephone her at 01 748 4824. While the Rose Ball crowd is far from stand-offish, and indeed notably informal as the night wears on, as we have seen, it's probably best to make up your own party and book a table. Wines are extra.

How to get there
You can usually park round the Dorchester off Park Lane at night; but these breathalysed days a taxi is probably the best bet.

THE FOURTH OF JUNE

MAY/JUNE

'As we waded through the newly-cut hay, ducking to avoid flying champagne corks, we passed several cocktail parties in full swing. Near other cars, boys and their parents were tucking into picnics of megalomaniac lavishness: buckets of caviar, cold chicken, salmon, asparagus, endless punnets of strawberries.

'Looking around, there was no doubt that Etonians, like tigers, are better looking. Most of the boys, in their black tail coats and with blue carnations or peonies in their button-holes, were extremely beautiful. Their elegance seemed to lie not so much in their clothes, which were often deliberately shabby, as in their bodies and the way they moved.

'The fathers were superb too – fantastically glamorous men in their forties, like greyhounds in greatcoats. And the mothers also, with their Knightsbridge legs and couturier dresses bang on the knee, were so sleek and glossy one would have thought the head groom had been polishing and curry-combing them for days.'

So thought Jilly Cooper, racy chronicler of English *moeurs,* on her first visit to the Fourth of June. Her verdict is echoed by the Old Etonian writer David Benedictus in his novel *The Fourth of June,* where the occasion is described as having 'an elegance, an ease, a pastoral urbanity; Sir Daphnis and Lady Chloë having *déjeuner sur l'herbe.* Cartwheel hats and brown Italianate backs and eyelashes like porcupine quills. Squadrons of stiff upper lips covering regular Fort Knox teeth; round, sloping, Chippendale shoulders and elderly young men carrying their paunches proudly like women pregnant for the first time. Truly we are a favoured nation …'

The Fourth of June is simply the open day of Eton College. It started in the eighteenth century as a gala in honour of George III's birthday and soon developed into an exclusive –

and then, a riotous – outing for high society. While much of what you see there is exactly the same as at other schools (exhibitions of craftwork and computing) and many of the events are perfectly familiar (chapel and speeches), there were always two events that made the Fourth of June different. One was the display of fireworks and the other was the procession of boats.

Any town that stands on a river is likely to take advantage of the flowing water for its celebrations; a glance at one of Canaletto's pictures of medieval Venice will convince us of that. The procession of boats at Eton is first recorded in 1793 and the dress still resembles that worn by sailors in Nelson's time. The oarsmen wear white trousers, striped shirts, blue jackets, and straw hats decked with flowers: roses, lupins, syringa, laburnum. Only an Etonian could wear flowers in his hat without a trace of self-consciousness; it is simply part of the mysterious, complex, and faintly absurd tradition in which he has been bred.

Yet the procession of boats only gradually became standardized into a ritual. The ancient ceremony of Montem – in which the boys paraded through Slough and held up coaches to beg money – was discontinued after 1844, because the arrival of the Great Western Railway brought thousands of trippers to watch the improbable shenanigans. The boys wanted another public beano, and the boats took over – though not officially. The river had long been out of bounds, because so many boys had been drowned in it, and Keate, the celebrated flogging headmaster, would announce each year before the Fourth of June that the school would be locked up on that day at 10 p.m. instead of the usual 8.45 p.m. for some reason which he pretended he was not clear about. So the ludicrous anomaly occurred that the king, William IV, could attend the procession of boats and fireworks, but the headmaster could not, and

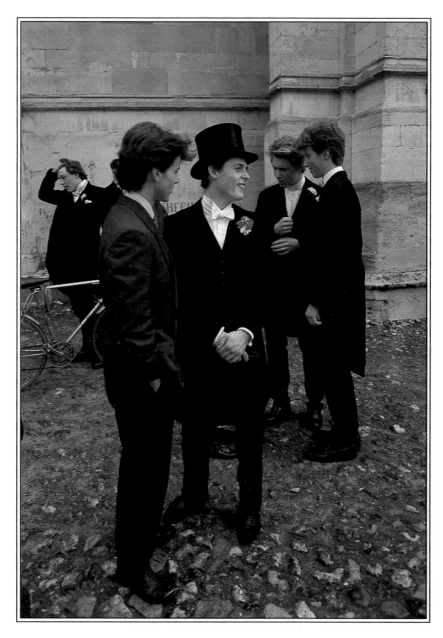

Above: Perennial Etonians in traditional clobber.
Previous page: Eton's answer to Interflora.

63

maintain his official ignorance. In the end, however, it was agreed that boys who had learned to swim could use the river; and the river has been the heart of the Fourth of June ever since.

'I went at 8.15 in the glow of sunset up the river to meet the boats coming down,' wrote William Cory, the Victorian poet and Eton classics master. 'The band – a vile band – played the old Fourth of June tune ... I thought of young men quartered in Indian hill forts, droning in twos or singly through a steaming night, miserably remembering their last row at Eton, pining and craving for lost youthfulness.' Insofar as any single human being could be said to have encapsulated that nostalgia, Cory himself must take the largest share of credit or blame.

It was he who wrote the words to the 'Eton Boating Song', that plangent threnody to the dear dead days beyond recall: 'Jolly boating weather / And a hay harvest breeze / Blade on the feather / Shade off the trees / Swing, swing together / With your bodies between your knees.' Few Etonians (indeed few Englishmen) can resist a pang on hearing again that bitter-sweet song, with its affirmation of a lifelong umbilical cord: 'Harrow may be more clever / Rugby may make more row / But we'll row for ever / Steady from stroke to bow / And nothing in life shall sever / The chain that is round us now.'

For nearly two hundred years now, the pageant has gone by. The boys and their families sit on the banks and the crews row by in their flower-decked hats. As they draw level they gingerly stand up one by one, raise their oars and lift their hats to the crowd. It's a pretty sight, but an extremely difficult balancing act, and many a boat is overturned in the process. It is romantic and charming, and a little mad.

The trouble was that a number of rich young Etonians would drive down from London in their souped-up Ferraris with their girlfriends, have too much to drink, and sabotage the proceedings. It was rumoured that some of the boats had been overturned by intoxicated underwater swimmers. So the college decided to end the fireworks altogether and move the procession of boats to the afternoon.

If the change has altered the balance between wet-bobs (rowing men) and dry-bobs (cricketers), the mutation is not visible to the non-Etonian eye. For the other great component

Jolly boating weather – and heaven alone knows how they stop the boat from capsizing when they all stand up.

of the Fourth of June is the cricket match between the school First Eleven and the Eton Ramblers, a team made up of old boys. All round the pitch the cars are drawn up in ranks – first come, first served – and here the boots are opened, the Clicquot disgorged and the picnics arranged. Yet even inside Eton, so apparently monolithic and upper class, divisions can be discerned between those who know how to get a ringside seat at the cricket and those who don't. Nor is the question of precedence confined only to the cricket field; it applies even to the Etonian ladies' loo.

It was the lynx-eyed Jilly Cooper again who noticed the principle at work: 'Outside the Ladies stretched a queue about fifty yards long. Tempers were becoming frayed, everyone was blue with cold. A large girl in buttercup yellow shamelessly queue-barged her way up to the front to an accompaniment of furious mutterings. "Oh the poor thing's pregnant, I suppose it's excusable," said someone. The mutterings subsided.

A red-faced woman in scarlet was baulked when she tried the same trick. "Let her through," said a ringing voice, "her son's batting." 'That's the Fourth of June for you.

It is yet another weird anomaly of English life that the Fourth of June seldom takes place on that day – in 1986 it was on 29 May. It's also the beginning of half-term break for the 1,200 boys, each of whom is costing his parents at least £6,000 a year for the privilege. On a gorgeous summer afternoon, however, seeing so many of those sleepy, graceful, assured and beautiful boys, all winners in life's lottery, it almost seems worth the money.

How to get in

The Fourth of June is a private occasion and you will have to get some friendly Etonian or Etonian parent to ask you to join his party. You could, if you were that keen, make your way along the towpath on the other side of the Thames until you are opposite the action, but you would not really be enjoying the unique Edwardian picnic atmosphere at first hand. Nor will you be allowed to take your own boat up that stretch of the Thames while the procession is going on. So it is really the old boy network or nothing.

How to get there

All you have to do, as one wit remarked, is to point your Hispano-Suiza westward down the M4 until you see a large castle called Windsor where you turn left. To avoid the traffic jams you can get the charming little train from Waterloo to Windsor & Eton Riverside station, from where it is just a short walk across the bridge and along Eton High Street.

DERBY DAY
JUNE

It all began as an aristocratic joke two centuries ago, but it has become the great English lark – an enormous spree on Epsom Downs at which all classes of English society dissolve in one vast kaleidoscopic blur. It is the richest race in the world – the winner will immediately be worth millions in stud fees – and it has given its name to similar races in many parts of the world, from the Kentucky Derby to the New Zealand Derby. Indeed the word is now used as a synonym for any sort of race.

It was back in 1779 that the twenty-one-year-old 12th Earl of Derby leased a house at Epsom called The Oaks. Whilst there, he and his friends decided to start a new race for three-year-old fillies to be run over one and a half miles. He called it The Oaks, and the next year a similar race was started for colts. It seemed natural enough to call it The Derby. As the great horse-loving statesman Lord Rosebery remarked, 'a roistering party at a country house founded two races and named them after their host and his house. Seldom has a carouse had a more permanent effect.'

By the 1840s it had become what the Prime Minister, Lord John Russell, called a national fete. 'I need not say,' said that keen *aficionado* of the Turf, Lord George Bentinck, in the House of Commons on 23 May 1848, 'that tomorrow is Derby Day. As that is recognized as a holiday in the metropolis, I have obtained the sanction of the noble lord, the first minister of the Crown, to my motion.' In other words, the Commons was taking Derby Day off. Disraeli, as usual, summed the Derby up most elegantly: 'It is,' he remarked 'the Blue Riband of the Turf.'

'For the first half mile,' writes David Holloway in his book *Derby Day*, 'the ground is slightly uphill and then levels out until the left hand turn where the course descends sharply (it is supposed to be the steepest hill on any English racecourse, other than the one at Brighton), rounds Tattenham Corner, and then into the fairly short straight which rises gently to the finishing post. It is this last uphill section which often proves too much for the less able horses.'

Why do people come to see the Derby? Not, Holloway asserts, because it is a better race than any other. 'It is the situation of the Epsom course, just seventeen miles from the centre of London, that gives it its attraction, and the fact that the rolling nature of the country and the convenient way in which the course winds round in a flattened horseshoe form make it possible for a very large number of people to see at least something of the race.'

Charles Dickens, a keen Derby patron, noted in 1851 the astounding logistics that already characterized the great race: 'To furnish the refreshment saloon, the Grand Stand has in store two thousand four hundred tumblers, one thousand two hundred wine glasses, three thousand plates and dishes, and several of the most elegant vases we have seen outside the Glass Palace, decorated with artificial flowers. An exciting odour of cookery meets us in our descent. Rows of spits are turning rows of joints before blazing walls of fire. Cooks are trussing fowls, confectioners are making jellies, kitchen maids are plucking pigeons; huge crates of boiled tongues are being garnished on dishes. One hundred and thirty legs of lamb; sixty-five saddles of lamb; in short a whole flock of sixty-five lambs have to be roasted and dished and garnished for Derby Day. Twenty rounds of beef, four hundred lobsters, one hundred and fifty tongues, twenty fillets of veal, one hundred sirloins of beef, five hundred spring chickens, three hundred and fifty pigeon pies; a countless number of quartern loaves, and an incredible quantity of ham have to be cut up for sandwiches; eight hundred eggs have to be boiled for the pigeon pies and salads.'

One young woman who very probably witnessed these gargantuan preparations was the fifteen-year-old Isabella Mayson, step-daughter of the Clerk of the Course, and a mere ten years later, as Mrs Beeton, to be the author of the most celebrated cookery book of all time. Another young woman, however, was to find the Derby not to her taste. Queen Victoria, just twenty, came with her new husband Prince Albert in 1840; but at that time Royalty did not enjoy their present popularity and, as David Holloway remarks, 'there certainly were crowds around the royal carriage but some of the shouted remarks were less than loyal'. Her eldest son, as Prince of Wales and later as Edward VII, in dramatic contrast, was to enjoy a long love affair with the Derby that began when he first went there in 1861 and was cemented when he won in 1896 with his great horse Persimmon. (He won it again four years

Her Majesty appraises form with an expert eye.

later with Diamond Jubilee and in 1909, with Minoru, became the first reigning monarch to win the Derby.) 'As Persimmon walked back towards the saddling enclosure,' wrote Roger Mortimer in his *History of the Derby Stakes*, 'the Downs echoed from one end to another with the cheers that were renewed again and again. Even the most dignified individuals in the stands for once let themselves go, and it was a truly remarkable exhibition of spontaneous enthusiasm and delight.'

The Derby has always attracted a vast concourse of people on the fringe of life as well as those in its plush-lined upper reaches. It is still a field day for pedlars, hucksters, tipsters, and pickpockets. There may be no gipsy fiddlers left, and no prizefighters; but it is still quite possible to lose your shirt at the Derby. Something about the high wide open downs seems to encourage a *folie de grandeur* on the part of punters. 'Does anyone wish to lay three to one against my horse?' asked Lord George Bentinck. When Lord Glasgow volunteered, Lord George added: 'Very good, but I don't want any small bets.' Lord Glasgow was undaunted: 'Nor I; if ninety thousand to thirty will

suit you, I will buy it.' As Holloway reports: 'Even so great a gambler as Lord George took fright at this. (He was wise; his horse lost that year).'

Other noble lords were not so temperate. Henry, 4th and last Marquess of Hastings, was born in 1842 and in 1861 inherited vast estates, valued at more than £250,000 and bringing him an income of £20,000 a year. Yet in no time he was dead, his estates sold to pay his gambling debts, most of which he lost on just two Derbies – those of 1867 and 1868. He ran off with Lady Florence Paget, the fiancée of a rich Lincolnshire landowner called Henry Chaplin. All that could be said in favour of Hastings was that he had saved Chaplin from marrying the fickle Florence. Chaplin took the loss on the chin,

and his equanimity riled Hastings into unbalanced plots of vengeance. In 1867 Hermit, owned by Chaplin, was much fancied for the Derby, but burst a blood vessel in training. Hastings, out of sheer cussedness, had accepted enormous bets on Hermit, and now stood to win a fortune. However, Captain Machell, Chaplin's racing manager, stood to lose a fortune, and persuaded Chaplin to let the little chestnut colt race. Even at this late stage Chaplin sportingly suggested to Hastings that he could back the colt at long odds to cover his losses if he won. Hastings scorned the offer; Hermit won by a nose.

Hastings now staked everything on his gifted two-year-old, Lady Elizabeth. She won the New Stakes at Ascot ten days later, enabling Hastings to recoup almost all his losses, and twelve more races; but her defeat in the Middle Park Stakes left him on the floor again. By the end of 1867 he had resigned from the Jockey Club, his Scottish estates were sold, and his stately home at Donington heavily mortgaged. All now turned on the 1868 Derby; but Lady Elizabeth had been driven too hard and was worn out. She trailed badly in the Derby, and in the Oaks next day, and Hastings was totally destroyed. His final whispered words were: 'Hermit's Derby broke my heart. But I did not show it, did I?'

Yet the most sensational Derby of all time was unquestionably that of 1913; and for two quite separate reasons. Mr C. Bowyer Ismay was the thirty-nine-year-old son of Thomas Ismay, a Cumberland shipbuilder who had founded the White Star line of great transatlantic liners. Thomas was succeeded by his eldest son Bruce Ismay, while Bowyer preferred to shoot big game in East Africa and to race horses. In 1911 he bought a yearling and named him Craganour after the grouse moor he rented every season in Scotland.

Above: Cold salmon and all the trimmings for those who can afford it.
Opposite: Laugh? Why, I thought I would have died – have you bought the street Bill?

Craganour won the New Stakes at Ascot in June 1912; but the brilliant victory brought little pleasure to Bowyer, still stunned by the loss of the White Star liner *Titanic* two months earlier. His brother Bruce and his sister-in-law survived the disaster; their manservant was drowned. Several newspapers branded Bruce a coward; and the stigma lay over the rest of the family. Next year Craganour seemed a virtual certainty for the Derby; and started favourite at 6-4. Three furlongs from home the 100-1 outsider Aboyeur led; Craganour drew level with him and the two jockeys were suddenly involved in a furious barging match. Craganour came home first, to the relief of the countless punters whose money was riding on the favourite, and was led in triumph to the winner's enclosure. The jockeys disappeared into the weighing room when an official burst in and announced that there was an objection. Yet it had not come from Aboyeur's owner, Mr A.P. Cunliffe, who was said to be the shrewdest gambler in the kingdom: he saw nothing to which he could object. It soon became clear that it was the stewards themselves who had initiated the objection; and as they were therefore both prosecutors and judges there was little doubt that their objection would be upheld. It was. Craganour was held to have come last for jostling the second horse; and Aboyeur was declared the winner.

The three stewards that day were Lord Rosebery, Major Eustace Loder, and Lord Wolverton. Since Lord Rosebery had a Derby runner, he could not officiate; though he was present when the evidence was heard. Loder was long thought to have had a vendetta against Ismay; and knew many people who had been lost on the *Titanic*. He died next year of Bright's disease, a disorder of the nervous system which can unbalance judgement. At any rate, Craganour's disqualification has never been adequately explained.

The 1913 Derby is also remembered for quite another reason. It was in that year that the suffragette Emily Davison, a militant member of the Women's Social and Political Union, whose colour she wore round her waist, stepped out from behind the rails as the field came thundering round Tattenham Corner. It is invariably held that she threw herself under the King's horse Anmer; *The Times* even suggested that she had tried to seize its reins. In fact she had almost certainly intended

Bus tops – one of the oldest and best ways to watch the Derby.

no more than a dramatic protest and the King's jockey Herbert Jones himself testified to the look of horror on her face when she saw that she would be knocked down. A rare piece of contemporary newsreel shows that she wandered rather than walked on to the course and turned her back on the horses just before being struck. She died in Epsom hospital the following Sunday. The King noted in his diary that night that it had been 'a most regrettable, scandalous proceeding'. His subjects concurred. It was only with the greatest difficulty that Miss Davison could be given a Christian burial; several clergymen refused to officiate.

The next summer saw the last peacetime Derby before the Great War; yet the race was still held at Newmarket throughout it (as indeed it was throughout the Second World War). The miracle is that so little has changed. A quarter of a million people still go to the Derby. Some now arrive by helicopter – indeed, with a new heliport in operation, they fly in every few minutes, bringing jockeys, owners and trainers who want to avoid the inevitable traffic jams. The Queen drives up the course itself but, for the great majority, road or rail are still the only solution. Since the Downs are free, it is the most democratic of races, with a thousand and one side attractions: a huge funfair and a whole colony of gipsy caravans; for this is the day of their annual reunion. You can have your fortune told by at least a dozen Gipsy Rose Lees.

The best way to see the Derby is to join the Epsom Race Club, which has about a thousand members paying a subscription of £40 a year plus £25 each for two guests on the great day. Morning dress is required in the club enclosure. Then there are the boxes, which now cost around £700 each and are obviously therefore in the hands of the big companies. There are 196 of these and the most chic is probably the one given free to the Home Secretary each year. And then you can simply buy a Grandstand ticket for as little as £10 which gets you into the Paddock for a good look at the horses. There are no dress regulations here, and in the 1976 heatwave some women came in bikinis.

But perhaps the most enjoyable way to come is on a bus. Some three hundred different firms provide open deck transport for groups as diverse as factories and London clubs. It is indeed a pleasant experience to leave London at 9 a.m. and bowl down to Tattenham Corner in the open air as if you were ten again, especially if there is champagne laid on to keep you going, and there usually is.

In 1986 there were two dramas of rather different scale. The first occurred when Miss Joan Collins, steamy star of the television soap opera *Dynasty*, elected to make her Derby entrance at just the same moment as the royal party, thus eliciting from the Queen one of her authentic Hanoverian glares. The second came in the race itself, when the favourite, Dancing Brave, owned by Mr Khaled Abdulla and ridden by the veteran jockey Greville Starkey, who had been enormously heavily backed, failed by half a length to beat the Aga Khan's Shahrastani. There were many long faces and raised eyebrows in the City.

One of the most famous paintings of the nineteenth century is William Frith's *Derby Day*, just as one of the most vivid verbal portrayals of this great English rave-up was painted by Charles Dickens. The *News of the World* used Frith's painting as an advertisement to go with a famous slogan: 'All human life is there.' At the Derby, this is no more or less than the truth.

How to get in
As has been described, the best way of going to the Derby is as a member of the Epsom Race Club, but if you can't manage that then Grandstand tickets can be bought on arrival or booked through Keith Prowse Ltd. Grandstand tickets cost £12, with a £4 supplement if you want to wander to the Paddock for a closer look at the nag carrying your money. For £6 you can get into the Lonsdale Enclosure where the dress is more informal and the betting more knowledgeable, and the cheapest tickets of all are for the Tattenham and Walton Enclosures at £4 each. Seats in the best part of the Grandstand, known as the Anglesey Enclosure may be booked in advance for £30 each. Car parking spaces can be reserved and cost from £10 for the best to £3 for the ones farthest away.

How to get there
Only seventeen miles from the centre of London, the racecourse on Epsom Downs can be reached by five main approach roads for those going by car. There is always a dreadful jam on Derby day so early arrival is vital – the gates open at 10 a.m. Railway passengers have the choice of three stations: Epsom Town, Tattenham Corner and Epsom Downs, all of which are within one mile of the course (and there is a special bus service from the Town station on racedays). The fifteen-minute trip from the London Heliport at Battersea (a journey which will give you fascinating views of all the motorists stuck in the race traffic) can be booked through the several companies now operating an efficient service to the Derby. CB Executive Helicopters (tel. 01 228 3232), for example, charge £150 plus VAT per person for the return journey – they sweeten the expense by providing strawberries and champagne before you set off in the morning.

CRICKET AT LORD'S

JUNE

Not the House of Lords of course; though many peers belong to Thomas Lord's cricket ground. It is the head-quarters of cricket and still manages to intermingle the most gratifying and exasperating aspects of the noble summer game. Its pedigree is as long as its origins are aristocratic. The Earl of Winchelsea and other assorted swells used to play cricket on White Conduit fields at Islington. In 1752 they formed the White Conduit Club; but, since they felt it beneath their dignity to play on public land, the Earl instructed one of his employees, a capable man called Thomas Lord, to arrange a lease of some private land. This he did in what is now Dorset Square. The ground was opened in 1787, and in that year some members of the White Conduit Club formed the Marylebone Cricket Club, since Marylebone was the parish to which they had now moved. The following year, 1788, the Marylebone Cricket Club played its first game against the old White Conduit Club, winning by 83 runs. The clubs then merged as the Marylebone Cricket Club, or more familiarly the MCC, which thus, as it were in a fit of absentmindedness, became the governing body of the game of cricket.

The first Eton v. Harrow match was played in 1805; Lord Byron was in the losing Harrow side. The first Gentlemen v. Players match was played next year. In 1809, however, the canny Thomas Lord, forewarned of an increase in rent, shifted his turf to the top of Lisson Grove; but five years later, since the new Regent's Canal was going to cut right through it, he moved to the present site. The first pavilion was a one-room building; it burned down in 1825 during the Harrow v. Winchester match and all records were lost; but it was soon rebuilt. The first Lord's Test, and the fifteenth between England and Australia, was held there in 1884; England won. The last Gentlemen v. Players game was held in 1962; after it, the old distinction between amateur and professional status was abolished; all players from then on used the same dressing-room. Then in 1970 the newly formed Cricket Council took over from the MCC as the governing body of cricket. Still, it meets at Lord's, and the ground is still the Mecca of the game. It breathes history.

'I do believe that the spirit of the past lingers at Lord's,' wrote one country vicar. 'The very air is impregnated with the game; and it may be, the ghosts of cricketers, long dead, gather there on summer nights.'

One of the oldest surviving cricket posters brings us back with a thump to the dear dead days beyond recall: 'CRICKET. A grand match will be played in Lord's New Cricket Ground on Thursday June the 6th 1816, and the following day, between TWO SELECT ELEVENS of all ENGLAND. For Five Hundred Guineas a Side. The Wicket to be pitched at Eleven O'Clock. Admittance SIX PENCE. Good stabling on the ground.' Lord Frederick Beauclerk captained one team; Lord Clifton the other. This same Lord Beauclerk had given up playing the game by the time Sir Spencer Ponsonby-Fane penned his enchanting memoir of Lord's in the 1830s; but he was still very much there. 'The Autocrat of the Club,' was how Sir Spencer described him, 'and of Cricket in general, laying down the law and organizing the games. On these he always had a bet of a sovereign.'

The betting aspect of cricket seems to have lost its way some time during the nineteenth century and has only recently returned now that Ladbroke's have a tent at Lord's for big games. The bets are now, in real terms, usually much smaller and the odds less tempting. There were one or two Englishmen who picked up small fortunes by taking 500 to 1 against England to win during the 1981 Headingley Test against Australia, when England had been asked to follow on, and Ian Botham strode to the crease to make one of the most whirlwind centuries ever seen in cricket, thus setting up an England win. (One or two Australians are rumoured to have done well on those enticing odds, too.) Ah, but that famous overthrow of all the odds was not at Lord's; though many another great victory has been gained there; as we shall see.

'Round the ground,' Sir Spencer went on, 'a pot-boy walked with a supply of Beer and Porter for the public, who had no other means of refreshing themselves. At the south-west corner of the ground there were large stacks of willow blocks to be seasoned and made into bats in the workshop adjoining. On the upper north-east corner was a large sheep pen. In the centre of the ground, opposite the Pavilion, was a square patch of grass which was kept constantly rolled and taken care of. No scythe was allowed to touch it, and mowing machines were not

Above: Members of the MCC discuss the play in traditional egg and tomato ties.

then invented.... It was usually kept down by a flock of sheep, which was penned up on match days, and on Saturdays four or five hundred sheep were driven on to the ground on their way to the Monday Smithfield market. It was marvellous to see how they cleared the herbage.'

The herbage however was not as lush as it seemed. 'It may surprise some people who admire the existing green sward at Marylebone when I say that within my recollection I could go on to the pitch at Lord's and pick up a handful of small pieces of gravel,' wrote Dr W.G. Grace (1848–1915), perhaps the most formidable batsman ever to play at Lord's and the man who is permanently celebrated by the Grace Gates at the main entrance. 'That was very detrimental to the wickets, as the ball would sometimes hit one of the small stones and fly high in the air.' There were, moreover, Grace asserted, no fixed boundaries at Lord's when he first played there. That was in 1865. In those days 'a ball would be hit among the spectators, who would open to let it pass through them, but often close again immediately. Fieldsmen frequently found it difficult to get through the crowds to the ball.'

Then one day a player called A.N. Hornby was out in the deep when a ball was driven among the spectators. 'As everybody knows,' wrote W.G., 'the Lancashire amateur was a very energetic fieldsman, and as he dashed after the ball he scattered the crowd in all directions. One poor old gentleman, not being sufficiently alert to get out of the way, was thrown on his back and rather severely hurt. The incident opened the eyes of the authorities to the necessity for better regulations, and as a result a boundary line was instituted.'

Thus Hornby was destined to an unassailable fame in any part of the world where English poetry is read and cherished. Big-hitting 'Monkey' Hornby used to open the Lancashire batting with the celebrated stone-waller Barlow. Both men were heroes to every Lancashire boy, and to none more than to Francis Thompson (1859–1907), the God-intoxicated, drug-dependent drifter who wrote some of the most lyrical poetry of his time, most famously a short piece entitled simply 'At Lord's':

> For the field is full of shades as I near the shadowy
> coast,

> And a ghostly batsman plays to the bowling of a
> ghost,
> And I look through my tears on a soundless-
> clapping host
> As the run-stealers flicker to and fro,
> To and fro:
> O my Hornby and my Barlow long ago!

Those lines were recalled by the novelist Charles Morgan in an essay entitled 'A Longing for Lord's' written in May 1943, at the nadir of war. 'It is not the game only that we see,' he concluded, 'but childhood and youth, and peace of mind in the recollection of enduring things.' At Lord's, he asserts, nothing changes.

'There is always the same freshness in the forenoon, the same air of hot endurance between luncheon and tea, the same intensification of sound and silence, the lengthening of shadows, the deepening of the green, and, it may be, suddenly an unreal tension exquisitely heightened so that each withdrawal to the pavilion is the death of a warrior and each new entrant a David come to battle.'

Lord's has a long memory, and is redolent of famous games played long before we were able to wield a bat ourselves. There was that agonizing day in 1870 when Oxford, with three wickets to fall and just four runs needed to win their annual match against Cambridge, had to face the bowling of Cobden, normally a fast, straight bowler with but little guile. His first ball was hit with a mighty crack by the Oxford batsman Hill, and all Oxford stood to cheer a boundary and a great victory. Yet Bourne, fielding at long-off, somehow got a hand to it, and the four became a single. So Oxford needed two to tie and three to win, with three wickets to go down. Butler faced Cobden's next ball, straight and well up, and drove it just as Hill had done. This time, though, Bourne did not just stop it; he held it, and Oxford had two batsmen left.

Belcher came in and took guard. Cobden bowled him a yorker. Belcher raised his bat. The ball shot under it, and shattered his wicket. Thus we come to one of the cruellest imperatives in cricket; for while by no means everyone in an eleven has to bowl, everyone has to bat, however indifferent he may be at the task. Stewart, *spes ultima* of Oxford, as the

Hon. R.H. Lyttelton later called him, made his way out to the wicket with thoughts it would be impossible to describe. He was a good wicket-keeper; but not even his dearest friends would have called him a good batsman. He had seen Belcher lift his bat and be bowled; he resolved to leave his rooted to the earth. 'Here then,' wrote Lyttelton, 'was the situation – Mr Stewart standing manfully up to the wicket, Mr Cobden beginning his run, and a perfectly dead silence in the crowd. Whizz went the ball; Stewart received the same on his right thigh, fly went the bails, the batsman was bowled off his legs, and Cambridge had won the match by two runs!'

A legendary bowler then was Cobden; but made of flesh and blood, unlike the great A.J. Raffles, slow bowler and gentleman cracksman, created by E.W. Hornung, brother-in-law of Conan Doyle (who once actually took the wicket of W.G. Grace – but then all cricket is one vast global village). One day at Lord's, Bunny, narrator of the Raffles stories, climbed to the top of the Pavilion to watch his hero bowl one of his finest spells. 'What I admired,' wrote Bunny/Hornung, 'and what I remember, was the combination of resource and cunning, of patience and precision, of headwork and handiwork, which made every over an artistic whole.'

Raffles might well have been well pleased with his after-noon's prowess. In fact he felt venomous. He had been asked to stay at a country house party to play cricket 'as though I were a pro myself'. But his revenge would be sweet. 'It seems they're going to have the very devil of a week of it – balls – dinner parties – swagger house party – general junketings – and obviously a houseful of diamonds as well. Diamonds galore!' And the two gentlemanly looters ride away from Lord's in a hansom for a quiet dinner at which they will lay their nefarious plans.

The Bunny–Raffles relationship is perfectly mirrored in the Mike and Psmith novels of P.G. Wodehouse; in each the loyal, staunch, rather plodding junior partner hero-worships the languid, debonair charm of his hero-pal; but for Mike the roles are reversed at Lord's and it is he who meets his destiny at the crease: 'Mike reached his century just as Psmith and his father took their seats...' Soon after that he is bowled ('Mike turned away towards the pavilion. He heard the gradually swelling

Eton v Harrow

Above: Greg Chappell at the practice nets while relaxing from the Australia v. England game at Lord's.

applause in a sort of dream.') Back in the pavilion, Psmith's card is sent in and 'a few minutes later the Old Etonian appeared in person'. Psmith suggests that what they both need is one of those gin and ginger beers. 'Remove those pads, and let us flit downstairs in search of a couple. Well, Comrade Jackson, you have fought the good fight this day. My father sends his compliments. He is dining out, or he would have come up.' Whether anyone still talks like that at Lord's is open to doubt; yet dream innings like Mike's still are made there.

Every cricket lover will have his favourite Lord's innings; but very few have ever been seen there finer than that played by Wally Hammond in the Test against Australia in 1938. In the June heat the crowd sensed that this might be the last time in many years that they would have the chance to see great cricket; for the war clouds were gathering. England won the toss and were soon in deep trouble. Barnett, Hutton, and Edrich were all contemptuously dismissed; England were 31 for 3. Then Eddie Paynter and Wally Hammond made a stand that took their country to 134 by lunch. Of these Hammond had scored a magisterial 70. He scored a second magnificent 70 in the afternoon; a third, perfectly symmetrical 70 after tea. Next day he added a further 30 before being bowled playing forward to McCormick.

'The enormous Saturday crowd began their applause before the bails had even come to rest,' wrote Ronald Mason in his life of Hammond. 'The roaring acclamation continued and intensified as he receded from the wicket; and then... the Lord's pavilion rose as one man and gave him the standing ovation that no one dictates but that is simply the instinctive corporate tribute of an admiring company to a performance that their blood has told them is worthy of this very special and distinguished accolade.' Neville Cardus concurred. 'It was,' he summed up, 'a throne-room innings.'

It was Cardus too who summed up the magic of Lord's in the evening after stumps have been drawn: 'Long after the seats and the enclosures and the Mound Stand have become depopulated and long after the last flash of white flannels has vanished...one or two intimate figures will be seen sitting in the westering sunshine, reluctant to return to the world. And in the stately Long Room, the old historical pictures hang on the walls like mirrors that have not only reflected but captured and fixed into eternal attitudes all the cricketers and cricket matches that have ever been looked at through the pavilion's great windows.'

The Long Room is still one of the most beautiful in the country; but women are still not admitted (except the Queen, who usually comes for a cup of tea during the Lord's Test and meets the players afterwards. Normally, though, she stays no more than a dutiful twenty minutes; as she leaves the royal standard is lowered over the pavilion.) You can sit and have a drink at Lord's, or talk to a girl, or watch the cricket; but you can't do all three at once unless you have tickets for the exclusive Warner Stand or are lucky in the draw for one of the scarce and costly boxes. They will set you back £1,500 as a private person for a five-day Test.

The printed posters outside the boxes list many of the same old names: the President of the MCC (two boxes), the Test and County Cricket Board (two more), the Secretary of the MCC (a fifth), D.J. Insole (a sixth) and Denis Compton (a seventh – but somehow no one minds forfeiting a box to Denis). Still, it is small wonder that there are so few boxes left for the rank and file. Business is the new force at Lord's. All those boxes that do remain tend to go to the big companies who increasingly dominate cricket. The list of firms taking ads round the boundary vividly illustrates their range: British Gas, Philips Compact Discs, Texaco, Ford, and Guinness. But then, it is as well to be entertained by big business if you go, for the MCC, in its wisdom, has given a franchise to outside caterers which stretches long into the future and allows them to charge steep prices indeed.

Thus on Test days you can avoid the school tuck food provided downstairs in the Long Room Bar by patronizing the Seafood Bar right at the top. It's pleasantly quiet and spacious, but they will charge you £6 for a plate of king prawns, £7 for another of smoked salmon; £8 for a poached salmon salad. A glass of Muscadet there will set you back £1.80; a glass of Chablis £2.50. Admittedly prices outside the pavilion are rather more reasonable; and if you take a stroll round the perimeter you will not be short of places to have a drink. First, there is the Father Time Bar, much patronized by Australian fans, with its Fosters lager, jumbo sausages, minute steak baps and doughnuts. Then comes the Cricketers Bar (more of the same), the steakburger van, the George Rogers stall with its sticky sweets, the fish and chips emporium, and the Lyons Maid ice cream stall; and next door, in sharp contrast, the red-and-white striped tent where the great house of Bollinger sells champagne and seafood to more well-heeled punters. They began to go to Lord's only in 1984 but they have already caught on; half a bottle of special cuvée will set you back £11, but their tent is full on Test days.

From here we stroll on and pass under the Mound Stand, with its new airy walk and railings set under the arches to provide a pleasant prospect of the world outside cricket; but no access to it. And then comes the Tavern, a soulless modern version of the charming old inn that used to stand there; but still a convenient watering hole for at least a thousand noisy and thirsty and knowledgeable fans on a big day. If, however, we are in a more contemplative frame of mind, we can turn off to spend half an hour in the Memorial Gallery, surely one of the most beautiful small museums in England with its plaque engraved: 'To The Memory of Cricketers of All Lands Who Gave Their Lives in the Cause of Freedom 1914–1918, 1939–45.' Then comes the envoi: 'Serene from change in their high-hearted ways.' Here too for your 50p entrance fee you can see how bats and balls are made; or study the little bag containing the ashes (actually of a cricket ball) which were the gift of some Melbourne ladies to the Hon. Ivo Bligh to celebrate his victories in the 1882–3 tour to Australia and which were later translated into The Ashes. Here you will see paintings of cricket grounds in Auckland and Melbourne, in Oxford and the Isle of Wight; and surely the only known cricket painting by one of the great Impressionists: Pissaro's study of cricket on Hampton Green in 1891. Lord's also now has a most professional library of ten thousand volumes to devour all through the winter months.

Outside again, we now pass the stretch of grass behind the pavilion; here several hundred picnic on the day of a big game, and here you can see several recumbent figures stretched out asleep who have lunched not wisely but too well; though to tell the truth you will very often see members asleep in the Long Room or even the Members' Bar when the gin-and-tonics have taken their usual toll; it is indeed this blend of somnolence and absorption, concentration and repose, that gives Lord's its special magic. The atmosphere on the Saturday of the Lord's Test is unlike that in any other sport. After all, the game takes five days and often even then there may be no clear result. So the pace is often slow and, at the most tense moments on the field of play, there are always ambling groups walking the perimeter or exchanging reminiscences in the Members' Bar. Conversation may range from how old Tubby got his promotion to Brigadier to the iniquitous cost of beer in the Dolomites (£2 a glass, would you believe).

My own abiding impression of Lord's is its friendliness. This may at first sight seem perverse, and in direct contradiction of its conventional reputation as the last refuge of po-faced blimps. While of course that kind of chap can still be seen there, most members of the MCC are simply cricket nutters, many of them young, and there's nothing they enjoy more than talking cricket to other chaps in the bar. What is more, I find it quite impossible to make the ritual stroll right round the ground without meeting someone I know. It is a great place for renewing old friendships as well as for making new ones. Nor does Lord's suffer from crowd violence; though the thirsty throng outside the Tavern can get pretty boisterous as the day wears on (the bars do not obey normal licensing hours and are open during all the hours of play, so towards six many fans have had quite a few). All in all, nothing is a more cheering sign of the coming of summer than the posters outside Lord's proclaiming the first game in April; and no event in the whole English season rounds off the summer with more razzmatazz, suspense and style than the NatWest Trophy Final in September. Anyone who still thinks Lord's stiff and starchy has only to attend that great cricketing carnival to see just how misguided he has been.

The heart of the thing, though, is the cricket; and the game is played at Lord's with majestic and maddening precision. On a fine summer day, with the sun blazing down on the emerald turf and the white figures moving over it in their intricate ritual dance, it is almost ludicrously like something from a boy's story book. Botham, for instance, may hit one of

Above: Well played Sir – the Eton v. Harrow game at Lord's nearly 200 years on.
Below: The new (or relatively new) cricket: a fan from Barbados.

his titanic centuries; then scythe through the opposition with the ball – he is the first player to have scored a century and taken eight wickets in a Test match (v. Pakistan at Lord's in 1978). He is the most charismatic player in the world; and one of the most wayward. Lord's missed him badly in 1986, when he was banned till August as a punishment for admitting to having smoked cannabis. (A letter in *The Times* wondered whether any of the MCC's ruling junta would resign for the much more serious offence of having driven a car at some time with more than the legal limit of alcohol in their bloodstreams.) True, English cricket was at a low ebb anyway. They had come back from their winter tour with their tails down after a 5-0 whitewash in the West Indies. They changed captain in mid-season; the elegant and gentlemanly Gower being replaced by the gritty and commonsense Gatting. Against the Indians England went down too, only managing to draw one of the three Tests and losing the other two; nevertheless at Lord's the fans relished Dilip Vengsarkar's unbeaten century and Graham Gooch's majestic 114 in reply. Later in the second Test series, against New Zealand, there was much to relish, from the dramatic switch in fortune which took the tourists from 5 runs (none from the bat) for two wickets to 215 for three, to the moment of pure schoolboy fiction when the forty-five-year-old Bob Taylor, drinking quietly with some business friends, was recalled to the England squad to replace the luckless wicket-keeper Bruce French, stunned by one of Hadlee's sizzling deliveries. Almost as if he knew he would be recalled, Taylor had brought his own gloves and boots in his car; he borrowed French's pads, trousers, shirt and box, Gatting's socks, and Gooch's (unused) jockstrap – and kept beautifully.

Up in the Members' Bar the chaps looked on, drinking their gins and beers but in no way allowed to take them outside on to the little balcony and stand them on the ledge until the tea interval. From such an intricate spool of shibboleths, of formality laced with informalities, is the exasperating thrall of Lord's woven. Collars and ties must still be worn in the pavilion, even when the thermometer hits a hundred; but a recent relaxation allowed jackets to be taken off. Ties stay on, though. The waiting list to become a member is still ten years; and there are still fathers who put their sons down at birth. It still matters that much to see the run-stealers flicker to and fro.

How to get in

Postal applications for tickets to the Lord's Test begin in early April and are usually fully subscribed within two months, the favourite day being Saturday. Applications should be sent to: MCC, Lord's Cricket Ground, St John's Wood, London NW8 8QN. Ticket prices for the 1986 Test were: Grandstand £14; Grandstand Balcony £12; Mound Stand and G Stand £9.50; ground admission £6.50 (children under 16, £3).

How to get there

Taking a car is pretty hopeless as there is virtually nowhere to park near the ground (apart from limited spaces available to MCC members at £5 a day), so the best bet is the Underground to St John's Wood on the Jubilee Line. Buses 2, 2b, 13, and 113 pass the gates to the ground in Wellington Road, NW8. The 74 comes to the St John's Wood roundabout in Prince Albert Road.

'Everyone who should be heah is heah,' the gorgeous people sang in *My Fair Lady*. In recent times there have been indignant complaints that many people who should not be theah are theah; and the *Daily Mail* columnist, Nigel Dempster, has said so forcibly more than once.

'What was once a graceful occasion,' he wrote in June 1983, 'which exemplified what Britain does best in the world, has become a sordid sideshow for naked commerce, publicity-seeking freaks and spivs masquerading as sportsmen.' In June 1985 he returned to the attack. 'Year after year,' he alleged, 'former jailbirds may be seen promenading in front of the glass front of the Royal Box – and last year I spotted enough publicans on the so-called hallowed turf to man a licensees' convention. So much for exclusivity.' His words raised a storm. While the man in the street might well agree that jailbirds should not rub shoulders with the Royals, a horde of publicans deluged the *Mail* with letters asking why they should not be welcome at Ascot. And indeed, there does seem something illogical when Princess Anne takes money from Croft's Sherry to finance eventing at Gatcombe Park, or the Duke of Beaufort allows Whitbreads to underwrite Badminton, and the man who sells these drinks in his saloon bar is made to feel that he is unwelcome.

'For many years,' Dempster goes on, 'the spectacle has been debased by the ludicrous garb of the Mad Hatters and those who have sought to emulate them by wearing extravagant hideous clothes more suited to a fairground. Is a topless Royal Ascot far away?' He claims that the new Ascot representative, Lt.-Col. Sir Piers Bengough, has made only a feeble attempt to curb the exhibitionists. His office telephoned the hairdresser, Peter Raymond (Mr Teasy Weasy), and asked him not to turn up in his usual bright blue or pink morning coat. But nothing Bengough could do has failed to curb what Dempster calls 'the extravagances of the ridiculous Mrs Gertrude Shilling', (the milliner's mother who for many years now has worn a preposterously large hat at Ascot).

Chauvinism is another plank in Dempster's platform. While English people had to ballot for the Royal Enclosure vouchers on Ladies' Day, he complains that foreign embassies, and especially the American Embassy, had no shortages, with two and a half thousand vouchers between them. He concludes: 'The seething masses have driven away the old Ascot clientele, to be replaced by a significant element of trash.'

It is the Royals who still set the tone. The Queen's elegant landaus are drawn by Windsor greys, with outriders in scarlet coats and gold-laced hats. The bewigged postilions wear purple, red and gold. The Royal Box, always filled with flowers, is arranged on two floors with bamboo chairs and panelled walls. The seven thousand people in the Royal Enclosure must dress according to the rules laid down by Her Majesty's representative. Women must wear day dresses with hats; men morning or service dress. None of this protocol prevents the 'ridiculous' Mrs Shilling from appearing each year in a hat which is so huge it makes it almost impossible for her to walk.

Yet let us not run away with the idea that Mrs Shilling is the only controversial figure at Ascot. Queen Victoria herself was actually booed when she rode up the course after she had accused a royal lady-in-waiting, the unmarried Lady Flora Hastings, of being pregnant; she had incurable cancer. However, Victoria was forgiven and went to Ascot every year until 1860, when Albert died and she went into permanent mourning. Happily her son Bertie (later Edward VII), a natural racing man if ever there was one, loved Ascot and put it firmly back on the royal circuit. Interestingly, as Dorothy Laird explains in her fascinating book *Royal Ascot,* it was his death in

Above: Ascot picnic: the yellow Rolls makes perfect scenery.
Opposite: Ascot: Them and us: but here even the onlookers on the
rails look done up to the nines too.

1910 that led to a mourning Ascot with a black and white motif so stunningly taken up by Cecil Beaton in his brilliant clothes for *My Fair Lady*. The truth is that a grey morning suit and topper, which anybody can hire at Moss Bros, will conceal a multitude of sins. It's not that Nigel Dempster is wrong; only that what he says is not new; not by a very long chalk.

The racecourse which Queen Anne had inaugurated in 1711 had been raffish enough during the eighteenth century, but the arrival of the new railway at Maidenhead in 1838 and the building of the new grandstand in 1839 meant that Ascot was now attractive to the town-dweller. The middle classes began to enjoy what had previously been the prerogative of the land-owing, carriage-using, horse-riding upper class. The Royal Enclosure, a rudimentary space in the reign of George IV, began its long development into the purlieu of privilege.

By 1868 *The Times* was bemoaning the decline of Ascot: 'It certainly enjoys in a peculiar manner royal patronage, and our aristocracy flock to it pretty much as they did a quarter of a century ago; but it has long lost all claims to exclusiveness, and with them have gone much that no doubt rendered Ascot the pleasantest of race meetings. It is a huge metropolitan gathering, retaining indeed some of the old prestige in the scarlet liveries of the royal party and the select circle in and about the Royal Enclosure, but in all other aspects an Ascot of the people.'

The question of who should be in the Enclosure, and who not, had not gone away by the time the pleasure-loving Edward VII came to the throne. Viscount Churchill, whose job it was to select those suitable, dropped applications into three baskets marked respectively Certainly, Perhaps, and Certainly Not. 'Now,' he remarked after allocating the precious vouchers for one Royal Ascot, 'I am the best-hated and best-loved man in the country.' His memory was prodigious: he once saw a lady in the Royal Enclosure to whom he had refused a voucher. Enquiries were made, and an interim injunction was served, forbidding a certain Miss Meadows from selling vouchers for admission to the Royal Enclosure. Nigel Dempster, kindly note.

The dilemma of Ascot's ultimate frivolity surfaced again on the outbreak of the 1914–18 war. Colonel Henry Knollys, late of the Royal Artillery, thundered: 'Is it unreasonable to hope that in 1915 the upper classes of men and women will forbear from assembling in their tens of thousands, say, at Ascot, peacocking in their plumes and prattling their puerilities, eating plentifully and drinking still more so, semi-intoxicated with the splendour and spangle of the gaudy scene ... while thousands of our countrymen are enduring every description of pain, peril, and privation?'

It is the perennial voice of the English puritan and was answered by the enduring voice of the English cavalier. 'The best horses in the world and the prettiest women are seen on the Royal Heath,' asserted Admiral of the Fleet Sir Hedworth Meux. 'We racing men go to see the horses, non-racing men such as Lord Curzon and Lord Robert Cecil and Mr Cust [editor of the *Pall Mall Gazette*] go to look at the women – and very good judges too. The incomparable beauty of English women is the real cause of the envy and hatred of their country that has been growing up in Germany.' In the upshot Ascot was abandoned for the duration of the war; its magnetic pull may be gauged by a report in *The Times* on 29 November 1918 (just eighteen days after the Armistice) that Ascot estate agents were already being asked what houses would be available for the 1919 meeting.

If the war had precipitated a social revolution, there was little evidence of it. The Depression left its mark only lightly on Ascot; the number of luncheon tents halved during the 1930s, and, instead of the usual queue for boxes, a few were available. The chasm between rich and poor, however, yawned as wide as ever. 'On the roads outside the racecourse conditions are disgraceful,' wrote Sir Charles Hyde in 1938. 'From an early hour bands of so-called ex-soldiers play on the roads, and trainers tell us the noise causes considerable trouble with their horses in the stables.' Yet there was worse to come. 'Unpleasant gangs hire blind and maimed men at so much per day to stand in the road, with the permission of the police, and they reap a rich harvest by putting their collecting boxes through the windows of motor-cars and begging from those proceeding on foot. They obstruct the traffic and are often insulting.... Foreign visitors to Ascot have asked us, "Are your ex-soldiers starving?"'

Ascot was – and perhaps still is – a paradigm of the

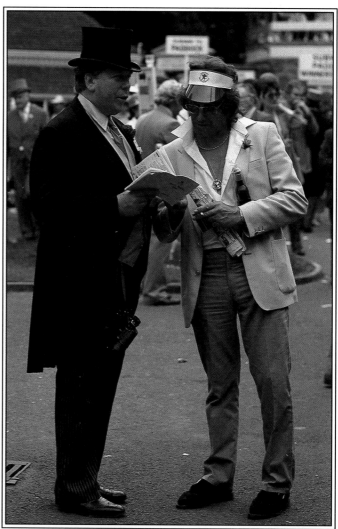

Above left: Ascot jockeys: the ones who have to produce the goods
while the rest play.
Above right: Ascot archetypes: the far-in and the far-out.

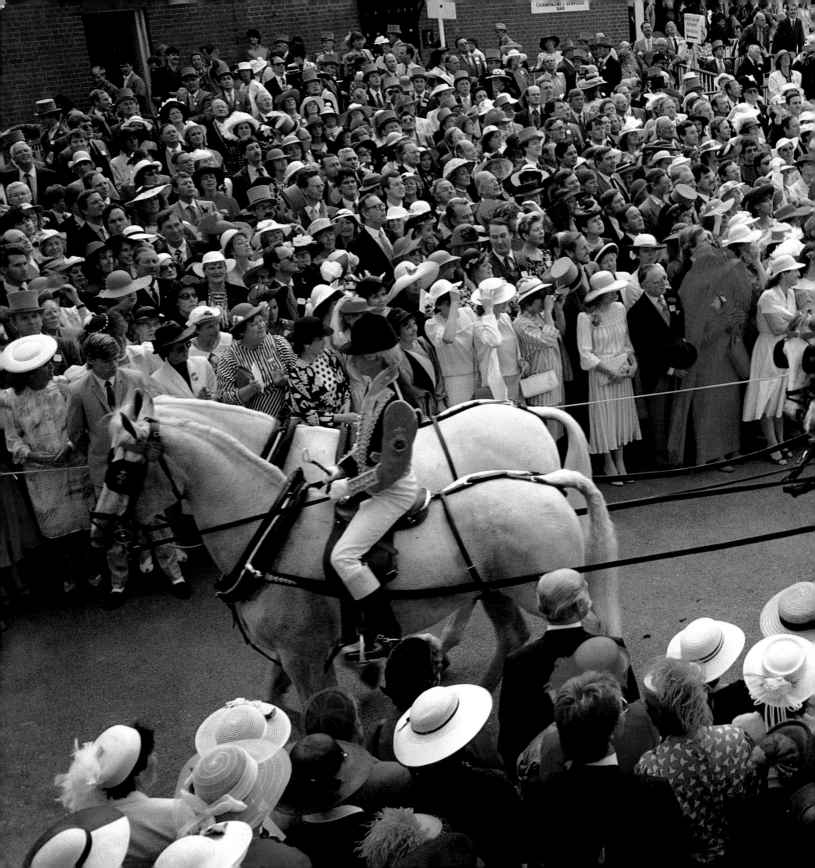

*Above: Ascot: and eventually, the racing – probably the best on the
flat in the English season (south of the Wash anyway).*

94

perpetual tension between the haves and the have-nots. It also has played its part in turning the one into the other. Mrs Helen Vernet, for example, one of Ascot's best-known characters, was left £8,000 by her father in 1890 – at least £250,000 by today's standards – and squandered the lot gambling as soon as she was old enough. She thereupon decided that there was more money to be made in taking bets than placing them. She began to take bets in the Members' Enclosure, and when the bookmakers objected, took the job offered her by Ladbrokes as one of their four representatives 'on the rails'. She stayed with them till 1955, never making less than £20,000 a year.

Yet even the bookies have had their scares there too. In 1965 the extraordinary Lester Piggott, then twenty-nine, won the Royal Hunt Cup on the Wednesday riding Casablanca at the useful price of 100–9. That set off a whole avalanche of doubles, trebles, and – what is normally known as the mug's bet – accumulators on Lester's five mounts next day. He started by winning his first race on the favourite at 7–4 on.

That was all right. His next race was in the Gold Cup itself, on a horse called Fighting Charlie, who had not previously shown his paces, but who won at 6–1, thus causing a slight chill among the bookmaking fraternity.

Let us now jump forward to Lester's fourth and fifth rides of the day, both of which he won at odds of 6–1 against. People with doubles and accumulators showed handy profits. But the race that would decide whether the bookies would really go to the cleaners or not was the King Edward VII Stakes, with Lester on his third mount, Bally Russe, at 9–2 against. Bally Russe was leading with a furlong to go, when Convamore, ridden by Joe Mercer, took up the running and went ahead to win by a neck. There was a stewards' inquiry, based on the suggestion that Convamore had interfered with Bally Russe; but the result was allowed to stand. Had it been reversed, Ladbrokes would have been a million pounds worse off. Even as it was, Lester Piggott is calculated to have cost Ladbrokes £350,000 during the 1965 Ascot – and that despite losing four races on the Friday after winning the first at 4–1 against. Lucky for some.

An Ascot crowd typically respond beautifully to the Kipling couplet that greets players going out to do battle on Wimbledon's Centre Court: they treat triumph and disaster just the same. A resounding example of the island race's capacity to smile through their tears was described with some panache in 1964 by David Alexander in the American racing journal *The Thoroughbred Record.* 'I have long suspected that the British are the last truly civilized people left on earth,' he affirmed, 'and this theory was proved beyond all reasonable doubt on Thursday June 18.' The rain had come down in such buckets that the entire card of six races was abandoned on Gold Cup day. 'Elegantly attired ladies and gentlemen sat dripping steadily, like trees in a rain forest, all round us. No one complained at all. They were in fact cheery to the point of being chipper.... A gentleman who had been shaking water from the brim of his topper for the last hour remarked, "I say, I'm rather glad you know! Let's all go to the bar. It's a splendid day for getting squiffed, isn't it?"'

Yet you need not get squiffed; nor need you get broke. A £1 badge will let you on to the Heath, with a thrilling close-up view of the racing from the rails. Indeed, if you have some binoculars and a transistor you will probably see most of the race and get expert commentary on the bits you can't see. A mere £5 will get your car into the public car park and, though there is a long jam from Junction 6 on the M4 along the seven miles to Ascot, once inside, there are acres of room for you to spread your tables and sunshades and picnic in grand style.

For those with a little more cash, £12 buys entrance to the Grandstand and the Paddock where it is possible to bag a stool and have a close-up view of horses and jockeys, owners and trainers. Or, you can go up into one of the galleries, place your bets, drink some Pimm's, and watch the racing on TV. The Paddock adjoins the Royal Enclosure so you can also have a perfect view of high society without bothering to get in there yourself.

If, however, you *do* have an ambition to join the Royals, you must start early in the year and write to the Ascot Office in St James's Palace. Despite an elaborate vetting procedure, as we have seen, some odd people do join the seven thousand jetsetters these days.

The great joy of Ascot is its dazzling colour and curiously informal holiday spirit. Although, for example, Ladies' Day is probably the dressiest of the year, you can in fact wear anything from crinolines or strapless black organza to pastel jumpsuits with high heels. All those are there, and all sorts of people: in 1985 ten secretaries had clubbed together to hire a mini-bus and drove there in style sipping from a bottle of the Widow in their picture hats – a kind of female equivalent of a football outing. Obviously the sun helps; and when it does come out there are few prettier sights than the lush green new-mown turf against the sparkling white buildings and the blazing flower displays. There is a children's play area and a brass band and, thanks to the numerous underground tunnels, reminiscent of a hospital or a ship, there is never a crush despite the crowds.

What makes Ascot so special for the racing man or woman? First, all the races are of the highest quality. While at Epsom there are only three races that are genuinely top class – the Derby, the Oaks, and the Coronation Cup – *all* Ascot races tend to be championships in their own class, and the four days arguably provide the best flat racing in the season. Then the actual physical nature of the two courses is very different. Epsom is a left-handed course, Ascot right-handed. The Derby course, as we have seen, is undulating; Ascot has a slight downhill start and uphill finish, but the straight is absolutely flat, and in the end a fairer test of a horse. Had the 1986 Derby been run over the Ascot course, for example, there is little doubt that Dancing Brave would have won. Indeed, he easily beat Shahrastani there later in the summer. It is a connoisseur's course, well called Royal Ascot; and it is a fine sight to see the royal party drive down the straight mile in open landaus at two o'clock each day amid a sea of doffed toppers and foaming curtseys. However, the royal presence is no mere formal duty; members of the Queen's house party at Windsor may well have been asked to join her in an early morning gallop along the course. Prince Philip and Prince Charles are more interested in other forms of equine activity and Charles for one has been known to leave after the first race to play polo at nearby Smith's Lawn.

But nearly everyone loves it; and if a visitor from Mars wanted to choose one social occasion in the year at which to see the English at their most festive and eccentric, he could do worse than make for Royal Ascot.

How to get in

Anyone can get into the course's Grandstand, Silver Ring and Heath by simply paying £12, £2.50 and £1 respectively, but it is the Royal Enclosure which should be aimed for and to get in there is a special procedure. The list for applicants to the Enclosure opens from January and those wishing to get in should apply for vouchers by writing to Her Majesty's Representative at the Ascot Office, St James's Palace, SW1, by not later than the end of April. Each application should include only members of one family and must state full names. Young people aged between nineteen and twenty-five may apply for a special voucher exchangeable at reduced rates but those under sixteen are not admitted to the Enclosure except on the Friday, when their badges cost £3 each.

Those applying for vouchers for the first time will be sent an ominous-looking form which requires the signature of a sponsor who has been granted vouchers for the Enclosure on at least four occasions in recent years or is known personally to HM Representative, Lt.-Col. Sir Piers Bengough. Overseas visitors should apply for their vouchers to their Ambassador or High Commissioner in London. Vouchers are sent four weeks before the meeting, and they may then be exchanged (at either the Ascot Office or the racecourse) for a badge which costs £56 and is valid for all four days or a daily badge which costs £23 for each day. The young people's vouchers cost £28 for the full run or £11 for a day.

How to get there

British Rail operate a frequent train service from Waterloo, Guildford and Reading to Ascot station, which is within ten minutes' walk of the course. This is probably the best way to travel, as the journey takes only forty minutes and allows one to be more liberal with the champagne. By car from London the best route is along the M4, leaving the motorway at the Slough Central interchange (Junction 6) and following the Windsor Relief Road (A355) and the A332 through Windsor Great Park. From the west proceed via the M4 to the Winnersh interchange (Junction 10) and along the A329 to the junction with the A332 turning left towards Bracknell and Ascot. For the Royal Meeting an early start is necessary and a reserved car parking ticket is a great asset. These can be purchased from January onward at a cost of £5 per day per car park, although the best spaces nearest the course go very quickly. The most convenient car parks, No.1 and No.1A, are reserved for Royal Enclosure applicants who have been admitted for at least eight years, and the car park is divided into numbered berths booked in advance. Here may be found at lunchtime the very smartest picnics between the ranks of Bentleys and Rolls.

COMMEM BALLS AT OXFORD

JUNE

An Oxford Ball, a young graduate theologian once explained to me, should be to pleasure what high mass is to religion. There should be something for all the senses – eye, nose, tongue, ear. In my day it was a bit like that: all that heaven allows; and all for a fiver per couple.

The idea of Commemoration – a celebration in honour of Founders and Benefactors – goes back more than two centuries at Oxford. Just when the young began to dance the night away to show their gratitude is not clear. Certainly charming old ball programmes still survive from the turn of the century featuring the polka, the gavotte and the waltz. In those more formal days a lady carried it with her so that aspiring young swains could book her for certain fixed dances at proper stages of the evening. By my time, the ball programme had lost its function as a timetable and become an unashamed prospectus of pleasure. Otherwise the heady ingredients remained what they had always been.

First, there was the breathtaking backdrop against which the comedy of pleasure would be played out: a medieval stone college set in enchanted gardens and lit by loving artifice to look its most beguiling. Then, it would be midsummer, with examinations finished for another year and the Long Vac stretching enticingly ahead. Then, there would be music, and champagne, and strawberries, and, most vital of all to the mixture, the very essence of youth: hundreds of young girls in pretty dresses and young men in dinner jackets, with the whole night before them and no duty but to enjoy themselves. Small wonder that the Commem was often traditionally the perfect moment for the consummation of first love.

And then there were bacon and eggs for breakfast, and punts on the river in the early light, and at last that deep and delicious slumber that comes only to those who have cheated sleep all night. So, in my time, everyone went to at least one Commem during an undergraduate career, and to that end a college would throw one every three years. Many went to far more than that, and not a few went over college walls to avoid having to pay. Styles change, dances differ, the music proliferates into new and outlandish modes; but the gatecrasher is still with us and no doubt always will be. Whether the actual quantum of pleasure changes over the decades or not is a nice point: I went back to a Commem Ball thirty years on to see.

The scene in the Front Quad of St John's was like a frame from a discarded Alexander Korda epic, provisionally entitled Merrie England and put away in the can when the cash from the Prudential ran out. The organizers told me that they wanted each ball-goer to say to himself or herself on crossing the threshold: 'Well, I've arrived'. First blood to the ball committee: we got the message. In one corner a whole ox was royally roasting; in another a barrel-organ ground out Cockney refrains; over here a majestic stilt-walker paced the Quad with giant steps, hatted, bearded and garbed like a latter-day Disraeli; here was a Punch and Judy show; there was Madam Norton Dwelly ('official clairvoyant to the foremost charities, including the British Heart Foundation'), a queue already forming for her services; there in the centre of a troop of rose-cheeked female Morris Dancers tripped their innocent measures, their great thighs and calves working with rustic rhythm.

Up in the committee room the American ball chairman, Jeffrey D. Wilson, said they had begun work the previous May and, according to his arithmetic, had expended 2,500 man-hours among the fourteen of them. They had sold 550 double tickets at fifty guineas each: some 160 to college members, 250 to people from other Oxford colleges, the rest mainly to friends and families. That gave them a kitty of about £31,000 for the

Above: Dancing to the Inspirational Choice gospel band inspires this kind of carry on.
Opposite: Will you or won't you, won't you join in the dance?

The morning after

whole splurge. About 400 people had been retained to serve the pleasure of the fortunate 1,100: there were some 120 entertainers, forty in the main bands, eighty caterers, fifty-three security guards armed with baseball bats, and twenty members of the college who were not, as it were, at the ball, but were helping out.

'For a ball like this,' Jeffrey explained, 'you have to win the support of the three estates of the college: senior members, junior members and staff.' His first task was to persuade the dons to let them have a ball at all; the collective St John's subconscious was still haunted by the nightmare of 1972, the last time they had a ball, when The Who were playing – their only date in England that year – and two hundred gatecrashers, mainly townees, ploughed the enchanted lawns into a Somme battlefield. Tonight, the barbed wire all round the college was ten feet high and one of the committee, a muscular, very fit young man, had had a go at climbing in and pronounced it unassailable. Still, there were the baseball bats on patrol just in case: a nice touch from a man who described himself as having been born a Maryland farm-boy. If anyone did make it later over that daunting wired wall, they weren't noticed and did no harm.

It was time for the second service of dinner in the hall: a hot, sit-down do, opening with a fresh salmon mayonnaise, followed by piping-hot home-made game pie, rounded off with the obligatory strawberries and cream. The grave and reverend seigneurs hanging in their oil portraits on the venerable walls gazed down on the candle-lit revels as the complimentary bubbly went down and spirits rose.

Suddenly two uniformed policemen burst in, as in some Ben Travers farce, and conferred urgently with Jeffrey Wilson. He rose majestically from his seat and asked us all to proceed as quickly as possible to the Front Quad, there to await further instructions: we had got a telephone message to say that a bomb would go off in a few minutes. It didn't, and by the time we got back to the hall the great Nat Temple, purveyor of sweet music to the quality these thirty years or more, was beating out all the good old good ones as if there would be no tomorrow: 'Our Day Will Come,' he crooned, as the young lovers slid, amorously clenched, in great arcs before him: but

their day was here and now. Meanwhile, in the North Quad, the Night-Club was host to the witty and polished warblers who go under the collective name Instant Sunshine: this was the only entertainment of the night that was too closely packed for comfort. For sheer proliferation of decibels, though, the evening had to be awarded to the pounding rhythms of the pop group Darts, their amplifiers shaking the foundations so that the whole grey stone edifice seemed to tremble under its 80,000 watts of floodlighting. After Darts, a blessed pause, and then the exquisite sounds of a Brahms sextet, played *con amore* under a lime tree in the gardens by a group of Oxford musicians led by the promising young composer, Anthony Pople.

Jeffrey Wilson took a turn round the freshly manicured lawns. So vividly had the imagination of the staff been seized by this ball, he said, that the head gardener, Alan Quartermain, had brought eight buckets of flowers for it from his own garden. And here was the head gardener himself, emanating from the darkness and adjudging tonight's shindig the best-behaved of the nine he'd seen since 1951. 'They're half-cut now,' he opined, with the expertise only nine such rave-ups can endow. 'Only half, mind you. What would be the point of spending all that money and not being able to remember what had happened? It's something you should be able to remember all the rest of your life.' There'd been no vulgar girls and smashed glasses as there were in 1968, when student unrest was at its height round the world and taxi-loads of socialites had arrived from London – nothing to do with Oxford, just there to make trouble. And then there'd been that awful night of The Who in 1972, when there were 353 thefts and handbags vanished by the sackful. He and Jeffrey were not going to dwell on those unhappy memories, though; only the bomb scare had marred the vaulting trajectory of tonight's endeavour, and that was safely over. Only two conceivable events, Jeffrey vouchsafed, could have halted it: the death of the Queen or the death of the President (of the college, not the United States), and neither appeared to be taking place.

Indeed the President, Sir Richard Southern, seemed ready for bed. We stood side by side and watched the strong-thighed Morris Dancers in a reprise: neither of us had ever seen girl Morris Dancers before. 'Of course,' the President said, 'the idea of men and women dancing together is comparatively modern.'

But it had caught on. Nat Temple had grown sentimental as the midsummer night wore away; the couples cohered and gyrated ever more slowly now, their faces and whatever else seemed appropriate pressed ever closer together. For those in more roistering mood, though, the legendary George Melly was now socking it to them in Canterbury Quad: a raunchy Pan in a Max Miller check, not a day older than when I saw him front Mick Mulligan's blaring trumpet in the same city three decades ago. 'Let's Do It,' he crooned to them, 'Let's Fall In Love.'

They needed no such bidding; and, in this respect at any rate, it seemed to me that nothing had changed. More of the girls now came from Oxford: the proportion of men to women had fallen from a daunting seven-to-one to a still unbalanced three-to-one; so secretaries, nurses and girls-next-door were still in demand. Long dresses, one girl told me, were such a rarity in the shops now, being only needed for grand occasions such as this, that she could find a mere ten in the entire length and breadth of her home town, Aberdeen; the one she'd chosen looked one in a million to me.

About one girl in ten wore a short frock, a few came in trousers and one in pantaloons. A seamstress was on duty in room F5/1 to repair the ravages of the night. At least it didn't rain again after the heavy shower at 7 p.m. – at the New College Ball many of the girls bore mud-stains to the knees after crossing the quagmires in the Quads. Here it was cool and cloudy and – ah yes – dawn's left hand was in the sky. There was still time to visit the French Street Café in Dolphin Quad and bid bonjour to tristesse with the plangent accordion music; to dive down into the all-night disco; or catch the University Blues Ballroom Dancing Team – surely the most improbable group activity in even this most eccentric and multifarious of all universities.

The egg and bacon breakfast has gone now – who wants to fry 1,100 eggs at 6 a.m.? – and the revellers were fed lightly but well on fresh croissants, butter and raspberry jam, with that greatest of all dawn blessings: hot strong coffee and cream.

In my day people tended to dine out and not appear at a ball until very late; with tickets at fifty guineas, that's gone. The dinner dreamed up by these young party-givers was, though, in my view much better – more skilful, more imaginative – than the sort of fare we avoided then. In my day you did not need five separate documents – your invitation card, a list of dos and don'ts, an invitation to a private party inside, another card to explain precisely where the private party was to be found, and, oddest of all, a yellow card inviting you to attend at Moss Bros in Magdalen Street to hire your dinner-jacket. Nor, of course, in my day, were there bomb scares.

None of this matters tuppence. The heart of the thing is just as it was: a chance to set the seal on your Oxford career in splendour. If you didn't enjoy Oxford, you'd be unlikely to enjoy that last ball; but then, in my humble submission, you'd be unlikely to enjoy anything very much ever.

I dropped in at the Magdalen Commem Ball to double check my verdict. The price of the ticket had risen to 85 guineas or, as we would now say, £89.25. The college of Edward VIII and Oscar Wilde and Kenneth Tynan, the place used by Compton Mackenzie as the setting for his great Oxford novel *Sinister Street*, is now co-educational; indeed before the night was out I had met two girls there who were the daughters of old friends. In return for their heroic expenditure the young pleasure-seekers were now to be regaled by no fewer than *ten* different bands, ranging from a thirty-piece hot gospel group through a jazz trio and the usual pop ensembles to a quintet called Night in Tunisia. 'After a successful tour of the examination schools,' the programme announced of this last, 'the quintet will be bringing you a selection of raw blues, calypso and soul, lightly sprinkled with some funky jazz.'

Silent movies were to be shown throughout the evening, there was a laser display, and in the cloisters marquee Annabelinda's were to stage what the programme called a glamorous fashion display. It must truthfully be said that the show did not take place because the stage collapsed; nor did the hot air balloon ascend at dawn because of the drizzle; but early morning shaves were being given from 4 a.m. in St Swithuns and there was a small funfair in the Grove with a Big Wheel which made me ill just to look at. For dinner there were *crudités*

*An Oxford Commem – and summer's lease hath all
too short a date.*

with garlic mayonnaise, *vichyssoise,* salmon, and strawberry *vacherin;* but lest the young tum suddenly feel the pangs of hunger in the wee small hours there were stalls, under the Colonnades where Addison had once gravely paced, selling *crêpes* and pastas. I was somewhat taken aback to see that these snacks were being sold at a pound a portion; it seemed a bit much after that £89.25 for starters; though, to be fair, money from a raffle during the night (first prize – two air tickets to New York and back and a weekend in the Algonquin) was given to, of all things, Help The Aged.

In the cloisters marquee with its striped roof and fairy lights and clusters of flowers and magic lanterns the young heads and arms bounced in Dionysiac patterns to Ken Lightfoot's Drum Boogie. By three in the morning, though, the revellers began to look distinctly dishevelled, their black ties hanging down in limp ribbons while one or two gallant fellows had taken off their dinner jackets and wrapped them round their goose-pimply partners. Balloons drifted aimlessly in the air and some people sat holding their heads in their hands. 'It got rather decadent towards dawn,' said my young friend Simone,

'but with Magdalen to hold your ball in, it just has to be beautiful.' My other young friend Frances concurred. Hadn't she minded that drizzle? 'But it was lovely,' she said to me. 'So beautiful.' And how about the funfair, that unsettling intimation that Disneyland had taken a lease beside the Isis? 'You know,' she said dreamily, 'from the top you could see the whole of Oxford.'

How to get in

Obtaining tickets is difficult if you haven't a contact at either university, but a letter addressed to the ball committee chairman at a particular college should guarantee you consideration if you write early. For an inside tip on which are the best balls each summer try ringing the undergraduate newspapers - Cherwell *at Oxford or* Granta *at Cambridge. They will probably be only too pleased to mark your card.*

How to get there

Driving can be a problem if you've got to face a long haul back the next day, when you will still be very tired and probably still over the limit, so the best way is by train. The journey takes just over an hour by Inter-City from Paddington to Oxford and about the same from Liverpool Street to Cambridge. If you think you will need a bed for what's left of the night you should book well in advance at one of the hotels in the area, preferably one within walking distance of the college.

It was of course a Frenchman who remarked of the Charge of the Light Brigade, 'C'est magnifique, mais ce n'est pas la guerre;' but he might equally have said it of Trooping the Colour. Its origins are older than the British Army itself, but today it is an enormously elaborate ritual dance of the British Establishment, much of it somewhat opaque to the children and tourists who make up the bulk of the spectators, yet curiously hypnotic in its intricate splendours. There is always some new visual pleasure in the shifting geometry of the drill and there is always just the chance of some dramatic incident like a guardsman keeling over in the sun or, as happened in 1985, a trooper being thrown from his horse.

In medieval wars, long before soldiers could read or write, each military leader had a colour or standard around which his men could rally on the march or in battle. It was therefore vital that everyone knew what they looked like; so the custom began of carrying them along the ranks each day before they were taken back to the billet. When the unit was away from home, the colours were hung from a doorway or window to mark the company's headquarters. It became traditional for young officers – ensigns in the infantry, cornets in the cavalry – to carry the colours on parade and into battle, and they were protected by colour sergeants – a rank that still survives. The last time the Guards took their colours on to the battlefield was at Inkerman in the Crimea in 1854; but by then the tradition of parading the colours in peacetime was already a century old. It has been traced back, in fact, to 1755; though the notion that it should also celebrate the sovereign's official birthday did not begin till 1805. Except during the Regency and the two world wars, it has continued ever since, gradually accreting its choreography with the years.

What the onlookers are watching nowadays on Horse Guards is a ceremonial review of the Household Division by their commander-in-chief, the Queen. The sense of élitism which pervades these troops and which gives their drill its fine edge stems from their historic role as the sovereign's personal guards, though each of the seven regiments in the Division has a separate history, and some are very much older than others. The two cavalry regiments are the Life Guards, formed in 1660 from the exiles on the continent who made up the personal

Right: Weeks of drill go into the final choreographic splendour.

bodyguard for King Charles II, and the Blues and Royals, an amalgamation of two equally ancient cavalry regiments. The five infantry regiments are the Grenadiers (known as the First Guards till they defeated the Grenadiers of the French Imperial Army at Waterloo); the Coldstreams (originally a regiment in Cromwell's New Model Army commanded by General Monck and stationed in the border town of Coldstream); the Scots Guards (raised by Charles I, confusingly, in Scotland for service in Ireland); the Irish Guards (formed in 1900 by Queen Victoria to mark the bravery of Irish regiments in the Boer War); and the Welsh Guards (formed as recently as 1915 so that all countries in the United Kingdom could have a regiment of foot guards). Let there be no mistake: all the troops executing those elegant manoeuvres are fighting soldiers. While the first battalion of the Coldstreams, for example, were providing the No.5 and No.6 Guards for the Queen's sixtieth birthday parade, during the 1986 Trooping, the second battalion were stationed in Hong Kong.

Each colour is trooped in turn; in 1986 it was the turn of the one presented to 1st battalion Scots Guards by the Queen in 1977; hence no doubt the Scottish nature of much of the music: 'Loch Lomond', 'Pride of Prince's Street', 'The Glaswegian', 'Leaving Port Askaig'. The Queen wears the uniform of the regiment whose colour is being trooped. She is supported by a veritable posse of royal dukes: Prince Philip, the Prince of Wales, the Duke of Kent, and the Grand Duke of Luxembourg (colonels of the Grenadiers, Welsh Guards, Scots Guards, and Irish Guards respectively). Behind them come a whole gallimaufry of ancient office holders: Gold Stick in Waiting, Silver Stick in Waiting, the Master of the Horse, the Crown Equerry. An equerry was originally an officer charged with the care of the royal horse; and the association between the British ruling

class and the horse remains to this day unbroken and quasi-mystical. Indeed, reverence for the colour itself has now taken on an almost religious significance; and the audience, many of whom are not even British subjects, are expected to stand up each time it comes by – four times in all.

Still, it would take a flinty-hearted foreigner to be unmoved by the gleaming cuirasses of the Life Guards and the tossing manes of their horses; the spit and polish of the foot guards and the razzmatazz of the massed bands. It is a ceremony both touching and faintly ridiculous; one's sense of solemnity is not helped by frequent bursts from the bands of 'Here's an end now to pastime and play, lad / Here's an end to your games with the girls.'

For the 62 officers and 1,550 guardsmen on Horse Guards, however, it is no laughing matter. For them the daily drill to prepare for the Trooping began six weeks before. Each rehearsal is filmed on videotape, then replayed to senior officers in an upstairs office at Horse Guards to sort out aberrations. Regimental sergeant-majors will, however, not be too happy with a perfect rehearsal; they want the men brought to perfection on the day itself. That day will begin with a 6 a.m. reveille and half an hour's physical training before they change into their scarlet and bearskins. Anyone who faints on parade will be sent for a medical in these more enlightened times and not automatically punished; however, anyone found to have been celebrating in advance the night before might well find himself on extra duties. For an officer to faint on parade is a worse loss of face; and it has by no means been unknown for a young subaltern or cornet to secrete ice cubes from the mess refrigerator under his bearskin to counteract the effects of an untimely hangover.

By noon the intricate ritual is all over. The Field Officer in Brigade Waiting who commands the parade rides up to the

*Above: The Royals in force as three generations applaud the
high tech drill.
Opposite: The Trooping is still a prestigious place to be asked to.*

Queen and says: 'Your Majesty's Guards are ready to march off, Ma'am.' The Queen assents; and rides back to the palace with her guards jingling behind her. Soon she will appear on the balcony with her family to see the RAF flypast before going inside for a well-earned gin and tonic. What we have seen here is the acting out of the Army's allegiance to the Crown. It is a fact of life taken for granted in Britain, while many of the attachés in the stands will have hailed from more volatile countries where military coups are all too frequent. The Trooping, on the face of it one of the more frivolous or, at any rate, decorative events in the season, is in reality easily the most serious.

Not totally serious, though: I have it on excellent authority (though not, let me hasten to say, present authority) that the revered colours have been put to less formal use. There was a tradition that a newly joined ensign had to prove his virility before his brother officers in the mess with a lady of easy virtue. The scene of the initiation was the dining-room table with the regimental colour draped over it. I asked one Guards officer who has taken part in many a Trooping how such conduct could be reconciled with reverence for the colour. 'It's just the ultimate dare,' he explained.

How to get in
The procession leaves Buckingham Palace at 11 a.m. for Horse Guards Parade via The Mall. Tickets are allocated by ballot and are limited to two per application. If you are unsuccessful in the ballot for the ceremony itself, your application can be included in other ballots for tickets for the rehearsals on the two Saturdays preceding the ceremony, but this has to be requested on your original application. Requests for tickets have to be made before 1 March and should be sent to: The Brigade Major (Trooping the Colour) Headquarters, Household Division, Horse Guards, Whitehall, London SW1A 2AX.

How to get there
If the finances for your day out won't run to a taxi, the next best way to get there is by Tube to Trafalgar Square, from where Horse Guards is a four-minute walk through Admiralty Arch and into the Mall. Horse Guards Parade is off to the left.

BUCKINGHAM PALACE GARDEN PARTIES

JUNE/JULY

The first reference to a Royal Garden Party at Buckingham Palace is in 1868. Before then all formal court events (they were called 'Drawing Rooms' and later 'Presentation Parties') were held at St James's Palace; but there is a record in the Privy Purse accounts for 1868 of the first 'Garden Party'.

Over the years they have gradually grown bigger, so that after the 1939–45 war there had to be two afternoon garden parties at Buckingham Palace in July; and a third at the Palace of Holyrood House, when the Queen was in Scotland during the summer.

By 1960 it was up to three garden parties a year in London as well as the Scottish one; and additionally, the Queen sometimes holds an extra one to honour some large international organization, usually one celebrating an anniversary, like the Red Cross or British Legion.

The Lord Chamberlain issues the invitations to some 9,000 or 10,000 people and some 8,000 attend each year. You cannot *apply* to be asked (unless you are from a foreign or Commonwealth country, in which case you can ask your Ambassador or High Commissioner). People from all walks of life are invited, from Ambassadors and generals to chairmen of Parish Councils and postmistresses; but usually they will be chosen because they have done something special.

The scene on the lawn behind Buckingham Palace on a garden party day is like a cross between *My Fair Lady* and *Cavalcade*. As so often happens in the English season, it is really a contest between the men and the women as to which will look more glamourous. You see bishops in their scarlet robes, beefeaters, African chiefs in tribal robes, nurses, air marshals, Canadian athletes in their red blazers, and of course a whole swathe of men in morning dress with their grey toppers (though this is not actually compulsory – a sprinkling go along in their lounge suits). The women show a clear generation gap, with the older ones in formal dress and hats while the younger ones may even go along with some flowers in their hair. It is an odd quirk (and possibly a sexist one) that a man can invite his wife and an unmarried daughter; but not a married daughter or a son. This is no doubt a leftover from the old débutante season, when finding a suitable husband was the name of the game.

The gates are opened at 3.15; but long before that an enormous queue has formed stretching right down the Mall; thousands in their best bibs and tuckers. If you have a chauffeur, he can park in the Mall; and there are often one or two parties who picnic from their car boots while they wait for the gates to open. Then the queue begins to shuffle forward and snakes across the parade ground, through the archway, right round the inner courtyard and finally out onto the terrace and into the garden. It is, of course, a gratifying experience to find such a haven of sylvan tranquillity right in the middle of London's traffic. There is a lake with flamingoes, and manicured lawns and herbaceous borders to admire. Two bands are playing, one at each end – on the afternoon I was there the bands of the Scots Guards and Royal Engineers respectively. The actual music is informal showbiz: tunes like 'If I Were a Rich Man' and '76 Trombones', said to be the Queen's personal taste (and indeed one senior civil servant recently walked up the red carpet to get his knighthood to the strains of 'Raindrops Keep Falling on My Head').

The organization is relaxed and efficient. An enormous line of apple-green verandahs shelter row after row of tables bearing afternoon tea. There are triangles of white and brown bread-and-butter, tiny buttered scones, cream cakes and – everybody's favourite – strawberry tarts. There is tea or coffee and lemonade and – most welcome when the thermometer is in the eighties – iced tea and iced coffee. One would like to say that everyone's manners remain perfect; but as the temperature soars, elbows are occasionally used to get that tea before the Queen arrives.

She usually appears just after four, accompanied by the National Anthem. With her will be any member of the Royal Family who is in town – on this occasion the Queen Mother, the Duke and Duchess of Gloucester, Princess Alexandra and her husband, Angus Ogilvy. Each member of the royal party takes a different route among the guests. The Lord Chamberlain precedes the Queen and stops to introduce her to various people who have been pre-selected because of some special service they have rendered the country in the previous year. Finally the Queen arrives at her own tea tent and *hoi polloi* can come up to the fence and watch her taking tea – a little bit

*Above: Summer duty for the Royals – the Queen and Queen Mother
lead the family on the Buckingham Palace grass.*

like feeding time at the zoo. VIPs and important visitors to the country are invited into her tea tent, while the Diplomatic Corps have their own tent too. But for the rank and file there are two hours to stroll in the gardens or sit by the lake or gossip to each other; though your chances of knowing many other people are obviously limited. The whole thing has a deceptively casual air and a security-conscious guest couldn't help noticing that a determined assassin with a telescopic lens could very easily pick off anybody present from a window in the Hilton hotel which towers over the Royal gardens. But no one seems to care about that when the sun comes out and the bands are playing. Everything looks orderly and secure, and even the portable loos specially erected in the gardens contain heavy mahogany mirrors and rows of hairbrushes; as well as a discreet tray into which to drop your 50p piece (or 10p if you are feeling hard up). Thus, in one summer, something like 30,000 Britons and their wives – as well as a host of specially picked foreigners – have the chance to feel that they have been the guests of the Queen. From her point of view, it is all in a day's work; but let no one doubt that it *is* work.

How to get in
Although you can't apply directly to Buckingham Palace to be one of the Queen's guests, there is nothing to stop you approaching any local organization that gets tickets, such as W1 or Rotary Club. Foreign visitors wishing to attend must write to their Ambassador or High Commissioner, preferably a full six months in advance.

How to get there
The most pleasant way to arrive is probably by Tube to Green Park, with just a five-minute walk across the grass to the Palace; but if you are at all self-conscious in your morning dress a taxi is probably the best answer.

Previous page: The Royals at work, for those invited, a junket in the sun, for those who invited them, just another job.

TENNIS AT WIMBLEDON

JUNE/JULY

If Ascot is quintessentially the Queen's home ground, and Cowes is self-evidently the purlieu of the Duke of Edinburgh, there is no doubt that the Kents have a corner in Wimbledon. The Duke of Kent, brother of King George VI, became President of the All England Lawn Tennis and Croquet Club which runs Wimbledon, in 1929 (while still Prince George) and remained so till his untimely death in an air crash in 1942. He was succeeded by his wife Princess Marina and then, after her death in 1968, by the present Duke of Kent.

Yet the royal influence goes back even farther than that. King George V donated the massive silver cup, one of two presented to the winner of the Men's Singles every year, in 1907, and his son, as Duke of York (later to be George VI) played in a doubles match in the 1926 championships. In the Royal Box dress is still formal and favoured guests are invited to take tea in a chintzy room behind it where sandwiches are served from a large round table.

On court dress is a little more relaxed; though a club official in the players' waiting-room is responsible for ensuring, not only that they are changed and ready to go on court at the right time, but also that they are correctly dressed. At one time dress was very formal: cream flannels and long sleeved shirts for the men (Yvon Petra of France was the last champion to wear long trousers in 1946) and plain white dresses for the women. Then the designer Teddy Tinling caused a sensation by introducing frilly knickers worn beneath provocatively short skirts. Touches of colour are now allowed, but the rules insist that players must wear predominantly white. None of this does much to alleviate the supercharged atmosphere on the Centre Court; nor do Kipling's lines inscribed over the doorway through which players pass to get there: 'If you can meet with triumph and disaster / And treat those two imposters just the same.' It is sound advice, for the tennis at Wimbledon is unforgivingly fast.

The thwack of tennis balls has resounded at Wimbledon for more than a century now. In the spring of 1877 the All England Lawn Tennis and Croquet Club started the first lawn tennis championship. A new code of laws, hitherto pioneered a shade eccentrically by the MCC (see under Cricket) was drawn up and survives to this day (except for such details as the height of net and posts and the distance of the service line from the net).

There was just one event in 1877: the Men's Singles, won by Spencer Gore, an Old Harrovian rackets player, from a field of twenty-two. Spectators paid a shilling to see the final. Nowadays some five hundred players seek to play. They have to provide the club with the fullest details of their track records; a computer is used to sort out which players go straight in to the championship, which have to qualify, and which will be rejected outright. The seeding process is used to stop leading players from meeting each other in the early rounds and knocking each other out. It generally works; but is sometimes defeated by a brilliant maverick like the German teenager Boris Becker, who in 1985 stormed through to win from unseeded obscurity. Still, an upturn like that only helps Wimbledon retain its position as unquestionably the greatest lawn tennis championship in the world.

In 1884 the Ladies' Singles was started, and Maud Watson became the first ever female champion. Her feat was made that much less onerous by the size of the field she had to overcome: just thirteen other women. In those halcyon days, it was a British contest with Brits the only winners; but in 1905 May Sutton of the United States became the first champion from abroad when she won the Ladies' Singles; she did it again in 1907, the year Norman Brookes of Australia became the first Men's Singles champion from overseas. Between the World Wars different countries dominated in different eras; each year during the twenties, for example, France produced at least one singles champion; most notably the great Suzanne Lenglen and later the celebrated Four Musketeers (Borotra, Brugnon, Cochet, and Lacoste), who in ten years won six singles and five doubles titles between them.

Yet we tend now to forget that Britain came back between 1934 and 1937 to win eleven titles, three singles in succession by Fred Perry and two by Dorothy Round. But the march of America began just before the Second World War, when Donald Budge won three titles in 1937 (singles, doubles and mixed doubles), while his compatriot, the great Helen Wills Moody, won the Ladies' Singles in 1938 for the eighth successive time.

The American dominance at Wimbledon continued well

Above: Waiting at Wimbledon: but it's amazing where you can
get to if you are patient – and know how.

into the fifties with such great champions as Jack Kramer and Louise Brough at their peak; and it was in this period that Althea Gibson of America became the first black winner. But from 1956 till the early seventies the Men's Singles was dominated by Australians (Lew Hoad, Rod Laver, Roy Emerson, John Newcombe). Still, the Americans retained their hold on the Ladies' Singles till 1959, when Maria Bueno of Brazil carried off the trophy. In the last decade Bjorn Borg of Sweden has won the Men's Singles five times in a row while Martina Navratilova became the first Continental player for forty-seven years to win the Ladies' Singles. The decision in 1968 to make it an Open championship – open, that is, to professional and amateur players alike – was inevitable. In 1968 Rod Laver and Billie Jean King became the first open champions. Total prize money that year was £26,150. The Men's Singles champion received £2,000; the Ladies' Singles champion £750. The current prize money is some eighty times as much.

Conceivably it was the entry of this very big money that led to the sharp deterioration in manners at Wimbledon in the early eighties as personified by the superbrat John McEnroe, who made himself profoundly unpopular by arguing with umpires and linesmen in a way that would have appalled his precursors in the halcyon days when the All England Club held its first championship. However, there was no such behaviour in the Men's final in the 1986 Wimbledon, as McEnroe did not compete. Further, there was no American in the last four. This, the 100th championship, was remarkable in a number of other ways too. It was the first Wimbledon to witness drug tests, and it saw the Centre Court début of a ball girl. For the first time since 1965 no player born in the United States reached either singles final, and for the first time since 1977 the women's final was contested by players who were both born in Europe.

The European renaissance was continued in 1986 by the awesome Boris Becker, who the year before had been not only the first unseeded player ever to win the Men's Singles, but also the youngest (he was 17 years and 7 months old). Was his 1985 performance a flash in the pan? His opponent in the 1986 final was the Czech Ivan Lendl, already winner of the United

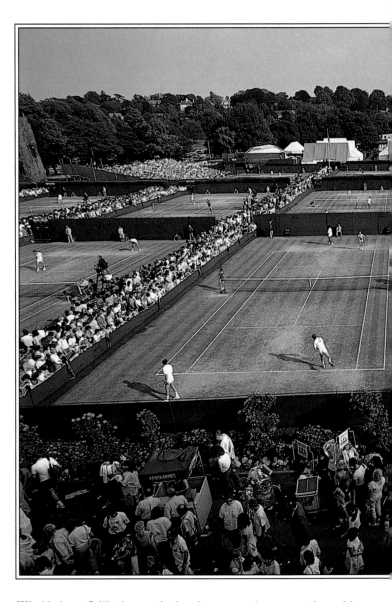

Wimbledon: Still the meticulously groomed mecca of world tennis.

120

States and French championships. However, since the French championship is played on shale, which is much slower than grass, it is not the best preparation for Wimbledon. 'If your priority is to concentrate solely on winning Wimbledon, you would have to skip the French,' Lendl remarked later. Nevertheless he began his match against the young West German as if he were an easy opponent after the Yugoslav Slobodan Zivojinovic whom he had defeated in the semi-finals, and he had three break points in the first game. As Rex Bellamy, tennis correspondent of *The Times,* remarked, however: 'Breaking Becker's service so soon is the equivalent of punching an Irish prop forward in the first scrummage of the match.' The nature of the tennis, he went on, was 'like checking who was ringing the bell more often at one of those fairground strength tests'. It was a contest with only one logical outcome: Becker won 6-4, 6-3, 7-5. There is, indeed, no answer to his 150 m.p.h. service; altogether he served fourteen aces. He is also, in refreshing contrast to McEnroe, a champion of great natural charm and diplomacy.

To meet the challenge of such super-tennis, Wimbledon has to pull out all its stops. The Centre Court and No. 1 Court are re-seeded each year after the championships and are used for no other purpose for the rest of the year. (There is just one doubles match played by four women club members to play the grass in, stamp it down, and get rid of some of the sap.) A second re-seeding is done in the spring, and the precious green velvet is protected by a tarpaulin weighing over four tons.

Despite its enormous responsibilities, the club itself remains tiny. It still has only 375 full members, together with a number of honorary members from abroad, who have given distinguished service to the game, and some hundred temporary members, elected from year to year, who are all active players. To be a member of the All England Club carries with it a rare privilege: the right to buy two tickets for each day of the championship.

Like many other sporting venues, in wartime Wimbledon was used for a series of unlikely purposes: fire and ambulance services, the Home Guard and a decontamination unit. There was even a small farmyard for pigs, hens, geese, and rabbits. But the war came closer in October 1940 when a stick of five

500lb bombs hit the club, one landing on the Centre Court and destroying 1,200 seats. Though play was resumed in 1946, the ground was not back to normal until building restrictions were lifted in 1949 and the war damage could be repaired.

The logistics of Wimbledon are formidable. In all, over eighty countries round the world and some 350 million people will see some part of the championships. The BBC television cameras provide nearly ninety hours of live coverage plus a late night review. No tournament in the world gets comparable coverage. Eurovision commentators are provided with thirty-three boxes from which to broadcast. The National Broadcasting Company televises the championships live for the American continent; Channel 9 of Australia and TV Asahi of Japan give the same live service to their countries.

There are some five thousand people employed at the ground during the championships to serve the needs of the 397,000 who will attend. In 1979 the Centre Court roof – some 220 tons of it – was raised on hydraulic jacks half an inch at a time by just over three feet to provide extra seats for 1,088 people. It can now seat 12,433 and provide standing room for a further 2,000. About three hundred umpires and linesmen (including some sixty women) are required to cover some 650 matches. For the first time in 1980 an infra-red monitor was used to help linesmen and umpires decide whether a ball was out or not. Such electronic miracles did little to dispel the tantrums of players like McEnroe. A hundred and three ball boys and girls begin training in early May in the skilled job of unobtrusively retrieving the 1,800 tennis balls that will be pounded up and down the courts.

Wimbledon is the largest single catering operation carried out in the UK. Over a thousand staff are retained to serve the 300,000 hot drinks, the 126,000 ice-creams, the 75,000 pints of beer, 12,000 bottles of champagne and the 18 tons of strawberries. The man who has bought the Wimbledon strawberries for forty-five years now, Edgar Berg, faces a major strategic question on the first Monday of the championship: will the English strawberries be on stream? If the weather's kind, the great strawberry fields of Kent should be yielding up their harvest when he goes to Covent Garden at 4.30 in the morning. If it's a bad season and the crop is late, he may have to buy abroad. In June 1983, for instance, he decided on the Sunday morning that he'd have to buy from sources in California. The telex went that afternoon and the strawberries were delivered to Wimbledon next day. Apparently no one noticed the difference.

The simplest way of getting to Wimbledon – though not perhaps the smartest – is to take the Tube. You get off at Southfields and the Fred Perry bus ferries you effortlessly to the entrance for another 30p. Getting into the ground is increasingly easy towards evening, and once in the ground, your chances of buying a ticket for the Centre Court get better and better too as the afternoon wears on – play often goes on till eight o'clock or sometimes nine if the weather permits.

Forgery remains a headache and there are other forms of con trick which don't even break the law. Two Texans told me in 1985 how back home in Dallas they had been persuaded to pay 1,000 dollars each for No.1 Court tickets – under the illusion that they would be seeing the top matches there. In fact, of course, it is the Centre Court where the great dramas are played out; and No.1 Court is, maddeningly, really the second court.

Some aspects of the season run through all the main events. Thus, at Wimbledon, as at Henley, jackets and ties are essential if you want to get into the Members' Enclosure. The same Veuve Clicquot and Pimm's bars are in evidence,

*Above: An ever frequent hazard: rain at Wimbledon. Yet
somehow, early or late, the games are always played.
Opposite: Wimbledon strawberries: for the man from Town and
Country, caterers to the greatest tennis tournament on earth.*

123

courtesy of Town and Country, a rather grand name for what is in fact Joe Lyons. Strawberries are now up to £1.50 for a small punnet (but perhaps they've come from California).

American visitors were thick on the ground in recent years but very fastidious. One American lady sitting next to me bought a ham sandwich and then carefully took all the ham out, leaving just the salad – 'I don't want to get foot and mouth disease,' she said.

Keeping up standards is a headache at Wimbledon as elsewhere. 'At the request of many members of the public,' proclaims a large notice in the main concourse 'spectators are requested not to remove their shirts within the Club grounds.' The rule is by no means always obeyed.

The sideshows at Wimbledon are almost as much fun as the action on Centre Court. In one, a game called Short Tennis was being promoted by the *Daily Mail* under the banner headline *The Search for a Champion*. Little boys plonked back services from the professional under the gaze of their admiring mums. And once again, business was much in evidence in the blue-and-white striped marquees. Hospitality was being offered by firms as various as Girobank and NatWest, Nabisco and Inchcape, Hill Samuel and Merrill Lynch. A small stall offered for sale at bargain prices tennis balls that had just been used in the tournament: here was your chance actually to own one that had just been pulverized by Boris Becker.

Even as the dramas unfolded, many hundreds strolled, gossipped, ate and drank imperviously. Inside the Food Village there was everything from smoked salmon to fish and chips and spit roast chicken to ice cream. Whoever wins or loses at Wimbledon, there is one firm which always wins – Town and Country. And there is another group of mercurial middlemen who never cease to thrive at Wimbledon: the touts. One of them, with the unbelievably apt name of Stan Flashman, was recently ordered to pay £3,000 damages to an American tennis tour organizer for selling £42 tickets at £125 each.

How to get in

The way most people get a coveted Centre Court or No.1 Court ticket is by public ballot – in 1986 some 400,000 people went to Wimbledon this way. To enter the ballot you have to write, between 1 August and 31 December, to the All England Lawn Tennis Club, Church Road, London SW19, for an application form, but they won't reply unless you enclose a stamped addressed envelope. The authorities have devised another way for spectators willing to risk going out to the club on the off-chance: ticket-holders who must leave early drop their tickets into special boxes and these are then re-sold at only £1 each. Thousands see first-class tennis they would otherwise have missed and the proceeds from this little custom go to the National Playing Fields Association. Even if both these methods fail you can still enjoy the general atmosphere by paying £4 at the gate (if you don't mind queuing for them to open at noon) and £3 in the second week. Then you can wander around all the outside courts and use the standing room for the show courts. After 5 p.m. admission is reduced to £2.

How to get there

Wimbledon is only seven miles from the centre of London and therefore within easy driving distance if you're living or staying in the capital. But taking a car means queuing for a car park and parking will cost at least £5 for those who don't hold debenture tickets. By rail Wimbledon can be reached direct from Waterloo or Blackfriars Station and by Underground on the District Line.

GLYNDEBOURNE

JUNE/JULY

Glyndebourne opera began amid derision and in fifty-two years has become perhaps the most coveted event in the social season. John Christie was a wealthy Sussex landowner whose family had owned the house at Glyndebourne for seven hundred years. However, he felt strongly that wealthy patricians like himself should put something back into society and so he began by installing a cathedral organ in the house in a large room he had built on for musical activities. Then, in 1931 he married Audrey Mildmay, a gifted soprano with the Carl Rosa Opera Company. He at once saw that it would be possible to give complete operas at Glyndebourne, but his wife saw that it would not work unless they did the thing properly. So, to the disbelief of the music world, and the derision of the press, they built an opera house which was ready by the summer of 1934.

John Christie really wanted to do Wagner, with the woodwind part played on the organ. His wife persuaded him otherwise and they compromised with Mozart, whom they both loved. Their first season opened with *The Marriage of Figaro* and *Così Fan Tutti*. Amazing as it now seems, looking back, Mozart at that time was not taken at all seriously in England. It was considered far too frivolous; but the opera was an immediate hit and Glyndebourne soon acquired a reputation for its Mozart productions – in many of which Audrey Mildmay sang with great charm and distinction.

The first three seasons cost John Christie some £100,000 – more like £2,000,000 in today's money; but the intervention of the John Lewis Partnership, and later the Hungarian tycoon, Nicholas Sekers, restored Glyndebourne's fortunes. It is now a charitable trust, and tickets are so hard to come by that in 1985, for example, there was a waiting list of seven thousand for Peter Hall's production of *Carmen* merely from the Friends of Glyndebourne, let alone the public at large.

What exactly is the magic of Glyndebourne? First, it is unique. There are other custom-built opera houses like Bayreuth; but nowhere else in the world has a private house been so skilfully converted to the pursuit of musical excellence. For the musicians, though, it is the rehearsal conditions which attract. Usually there are five uninterrupted weeks – unique in the opera world – for a new production. In other big opera houses, the stars may jet in from all over the world and have only six hours together before performing. Then, Glyndebourne quickly got a reputation for finding new young talent. Young singers nowadays usually go to their audition there straight from college to join the celebrated Glyndebourne chorus (past members include Peter Pears and Janet Baker). The best among them will understudy the great stars of the festival, then go on the tour that follows singing the roles themselves.

Besides, the setting is idyllic. John Christie laid it down from the beginning that Glyndebourne should be an event for which people dressed up; and there is no more singular sight in London than to see the Glyndebourne train leaving Victoria at 2.50 p.m. full of men in dinner jackets and women in evening dress. In this apparently alienated behaviour the train travellers show sound sense; for the road journey is boring in the extreme for the first hour though it then becomes a sylvan delight. On the other hand, whatever the comfort of the train, it is not practical to take on board all the accoutrements you need for a Glyndebourne picnic, and that is a *sine qua non* of the experience. Apart from your hampers of smoked salmon and strawberries, Pimm's and Veuve Clicquot, you may well opt for the tables and chairs which are increasingly favoured nowadays; and for these you do need a car. The best of all possible options is a chauffeur-driven Rolls; given, of course, that money is no object. Allow a good three hours for the journey from the time you cross the Thames. Or, better still, stay locally, and avoid the long slog home which may just take the edge off the perfection of your evening.

You need all that time allowed by your afternoon off from the city's cares to take in all Glyndebourne's delights. You may want to stroll by the lake, or admire its perfect English gardens; the herbaceous borders, the rambling roses, the water lilies, the backdrop of ancient trees, and the ha-ha that cunningly allows you to contemplate the grazing cows (and vice versa) without having them wander over to poach your picnic. You also need to be there early to park your picnic in a favoured spot and float your bottles of bubbly to cool in the water so that they are waiting for you when you emerge for the seventy-five minute 'long' interval.

This again is unique to Glyndebourne. Since opera is a long

Above: Idomeneo at Glyndebourne: it is hard to believe – but true – that Mozart was thought too frivolous when the Christies began fifty years ago. Previous page: The Glyndebourne picnic.

129

business anyway (*Figaro* takes nearly four hours) and the human brain cannot digest music hour after hour, some sort of break is necessary. The Glyndebourne picnic is the perfect answer. It is one of the less happy consequences of all this glorious indulgence that a few visitors doze in the first half, exhausted by the drive and pre-performance champagne, thus wasting the very large sums they have expended. They are usually, however, pretty much alive in the second half. Tickets now run up to £46 each; and are in such demand that there are even stories of their being stolen from the post. There is certainly a black market in them.

A Glyndebourne first night is a star-strewn occasion, with Friends of the Festival and Arts Council supremos there in force and critics from all over the world; but for the young singers just as testing an evening is the open dress rehearsal, when they know that the theatre will be packed with agents and managers, friends and cognoscenti, so that even the best rehearsed singer feels nervous.

But Glyndebourne is not merely a musical treat: it is also a visual one. Scrupulous attention is paid to the sets and lighting, and artists like Oliver Messel, Osbert Lancaster, John Piper, David Hockney, John Bury and John Gunter have all lent their great skills to providing magical designs. However, in the end the music is the thing, and it's the concentration of high talent that gives Glyndebourne its particular thrill. In the 1986 season, for example, Peter Hall was in charge of *Simon Boccanegra* (the launching of a new Verdi cycle), and Trevor Nunn of Gershwin's *Porgy and Bess*. Bernard Haitink conducted the first, and the young maestro Simon Rattle the latter. Obviously, for the heads of the National Theatre and Royal Shakespeare Company, Hall and Nunn, to be in charge of

an opera each is a unique confrontation of high talent.

It certainly paid off in 1986, if a shade unevenly. *Simon Boccanegra* was well received; but overshadowed by the *succès fou* of *Porgy and Bess*. There were those rarefied spirits who held that Gershwin was merely a minor composer who had written nothing more than a folk opera. Such malcontents had never heard it conducted by Simon Rattle and played by the LPO. In the event it was, wrote the respected *Spectator* critic Rodney Milnes, 'one of the most stirring events of an opera-going lifetime…an overwhelming, unforgettable performance.' The audience 'rose to a man to give the performers a standing ovation, something I have not seen in Sussex before.' Such is the hypnotic spell of the Glyndebourne experience.

How to get in

This is undoubtedly the hardest trick in the long cycle of the English season. The 5,000 members of the Glyndebourne Festival Society have priority in the rush to book seats, but as membership of the Society is at a premium (there are 6,000 on the waiting list) the only way to get tickets is by making very early postal bookings to the Box Office Manager, Glyndebourne, near Lewes, East Sussex. Enclose a stamped addressed envelope. Because the Society's members are asked to book so far in advance (by the end of January) there's just the possibility of returned tickets, which the Glyndebourne Information Office (tel. 0273 812321) are happy to advise on.

How to get there

Glyndebourne is in East Sussex and is fifty-four miles from London. The traditional way to travel used to be by train from Victoria to the tiny station of Glynde, but now trains go to Lewes station, where special coaches ferry opera lovers to Glyndebourne. The journey from London to Lewes takes about an hour. By car, the recommended route to the opera house from London is via the A23 which turns into the M23, returning to the A23. After entering the Brighton boundary follow signs to Lewes via the A27, then take the A26 Tonbridge Wells road, until you reach the B2192. Then it's a matter of watching for the signs and listening for those warbling sopranos.

POLO AT WINDSOR

JUNE / JULY

The point about polo is that, while anybody can watch, not everyone can play: the cost is prohibitive and that's why the England team usually contains the names of such swells as Lord Charles Beresford and HRH The Prince of Wales. A typical game will be six chukkas long, but simple arithmetic will show that as there are four players in each team and you change your pony after each chukka no fewer than forty-eight are needed per game – double that for an afternoon's sport, when there are usually two matches.

Polo clubs in England fall into two categories. The smart clubs are Cirencester, Cowdray and Windsor – the last being the mecca of a certain type of player known as the castle creeper. The unsmart clubs are Kirtlington, Taunton and Tidworth. Smart clubs are run for the benefit of the patrons; unsmart clubs don't have patrons.

The role of the patron is essential, for it is he who pays the substantial sums needed to hire lusty young men from Mexico, Chile and other South American countries to play for his team and thus, with luck, enable him to receive a cup from a royal hand. The cost of these 'hired assassins', as they are known in polo circles, is a closely guarded secret; but certainly the hired player will expect at least his air fare, a car, house, ponies, equipment, a cash bonus and generous fringe benefits. They may well amount in all to £100,000 a year.

For the wealthy patron the ultimate thrill is to play at No.1 himself with three excellent – and well-rewarded – players behind him. Three ingredients are usually held to make a man a good polo player: his pony, which is forty per cent of the battle; his eye for hitting a ball, another forty per cent; and his riding ability, the last twenty per cent. Eye is all-important; you can be taught to ride, but nothing will give you a good eye if you were not endowed with one.

It is not only the players that are so expensive. It costs £3,000, including customs tariffs, to bring a polo pony from South America for the season; a player bringing eight would therefore have to meet a bill of £24,000 before he had even set foot in this country. The patron will guarantee to buy them at the end of the season if all else fails. In fact the best ponies are still English thoroughbreds; but they take a lot of training. Perhaps the word pony deserves a little clarification: before the

Right: Polo – this most pricy and aristocratic of all English summer games provides unrelentingly fast, tough action.

First World War the limit to the size of any horse playing polo was 13½ hands (one hand being four inches); after the war the limit was swept away and horses of any size could be used; but the word pony stuck. They start to play at four to five years old; are normally twelve to fourteen, but continue if well husbanded to sixteen or eighteen; indeed some ponies have played well into their twenties. All polo ponies take the field with all four legs bandaged as a defence against swinging sticks and whizzing balls; even so they are sometimes injured and occasionally have to be put down on the field; a distressing moment for players and spectators alike.

Two mounted umpires control a game of polo, dividing the field diagonally between them, with a referee in the stand to whom they will trot over for a decision if they disagree. All fouls in polo turn on only one question: was it dangerous or not? Offside, for example, does not exist. Those interested in the finer points might like to read a book called *Polo by Marco* – an unlikely pseudonym for Earl Mountbatten. It is Prince Philip and his son Charles who have of course given polo its great modern *cachet*. 'I cannot help feeling,' Prince Charles has remarked 'that there are few team games in existence to rival polo for sheer excitement, speed, and fascination.'

The apogee of the polo year is International Polo Day at the Guards Polo Club in Windsor Great Park. The modern game began on the north-east frontier of India in 1859, heyday of the British Raj, and when you arrive at Smith's Lawn, where the Guards Club is based, you could be forgiven for feeling you had been transported back to the north-east frontier. The field is a great green sward against which the Lifeguards and the Blues and Royals parade at their most dashing. The Royal Box is a discreet but elegant little white structure from which the Queen likes to watch Charles, a classical, unselfish team player, whack goals for his country.

The game itself is extraordinarily tough, fast and physical, but easy to understand; and the skills are of a very high order. Notice, for example, how a top player can actually intercept a ball in mid air with his polo stick, after it has been whacked at goal from a penalty spot, as if he were making a return at tennis. There are about five hundred polo players in England; but the cosmopolitan excitement is provided by visiting teams from abroad – most of the star players are South American, but nowadays there are also some New Zealanders in the top class.

Even in polo, business obtrudes, and in the hospitality tents many a firm entertains businessmen and their wives from Australia, America, Africa and the Middle East. They will be wined and dined in a huge, airy tent with each party separated from the next by low white fences, and emerald green grass under foot. The menu is provided yet again by our old friends Town and Country, the upmarket name for Joe Lyons, so that the hordes of pretty girls, jolly Nigerians and ten-a-penny Ambassadors are well lubricated when they are called from the table by the ringing of the great bell for the first chukka.

It is a club every bit as glamorous as a Glyndebourne audience; yet subtly less intelligent and more moneyed. To do the thing in style you really need a badge that will take you into the Guards Club enclosure for the ubiquitous bubbly and Pimm's; but there is nothing to stop you paying a couple of pounds to park your car and watch from the sidelines. Windsor is essentially Guards territory; and the polite stewards who doff their black bowlers as HRH arrives in his Aston Martin are Guards NCOs in disguise. It is perhaps the most royal of all sports.

How to get in
All clubs have a public admission charge, between £2 and £6, and all have car parking facilities very close to their grounds. Polo enthusiasts can apply for membership to the three main clubs, which offers free entrance to matches for the entire season for the member, his car and a guest. The most popular club is the Guards Polo Club in Windsor Great Park, with some 1,100 non-playing members. Annual membership there costs £100, with a £20 joining fee. Details of fixtures can be found in the Yearbook published by the Hurlingham Polo Association, which is available at £4.50 from the HPA, Ambersham Farm, Ambersham, Midhurst, Sussex (tel. 07985 277). The three well-known clubs are:
Cirencester Park Polo Club, Cirencester Park, Gloucestershire
  (tel. 0285 3225);
Cowdray Park Polo Club, Cowdray Park, Midhurst, Sussex
  (tel. 073081 3257);
The Guards Polo Club, Windsor Great Park, Englefield Green, Egham, Surrey
  (tel. 0784 34212).

How to get there
The Secretary of each club is most helpful, and the best method if planning to drive to a match is to ring the club beforehand and ask for directions. All three major clubs are within two hours' driving time from London.

Read all about it
The Polo Times, The Manor House, Houghton, Stockbridge, Hampshire (tel. 07947 854). Editor: Colin Cross.

HENLEY REGATTA

JULY

The whole of the English season, as we have said, may perhaps be most elegantly defined as the sum of all those parties to which the English wear fancy dress; and nowhere is this singular penchant more in evidence than at the Henley Regatta.

Until recently, too, it seemed to have avoided that coarsening which follows when the big money comes in and sponsors' names are splashed everywhere, as has happened at Wimbledon, Royal Ascot and even Lord's.

Yet before we consider the nature of modern Henley we have first to disentangle three distinct entities which tend to blur in the English mind and all of which contribute to the public perception of Henley. There is first, the town, which nearly 150 years ago decided to use its gorgeous and unique stretch of straight river to launch a regatta. In those early days Oxford undergraduates were not supposed to take part, and those who did were not permitted to stand for fellowships, or be given references for holy orders. However, the arrival of Prince Albert in 1851 gave Henley the royal thumbs-up and his son, the future Edward VII, confirmed the accolade by attending in 1887. Our present Queen prefers horses to boats, but the royal connection continued with Prince Andrew presenting the prizes in 1985 (though not in 1986 when Lord Hunt, conqueror of Everest, did the honours).

The town, however, which still runs the firework display on Saturday night, long ago ceded its right to run the rowing to a self-governing body called the Stewards of Henley Royal Regatta. This, the second entity at Henley, is entirely non-commercial: it accepts no sponsorship, allows no advertising, and runs the whole show at a handsome pre-tax profit (£265,000 in 1985), simply on what income it can derive from tickets, car parks and bar takings. No one is paid to work at Henley; you may well find a peer of the realm looking after the lavatories. Though Henley has grown to many times its pre-war size it still is, to those veterans who can remember it fifty years ago, very much what it was: an Edwardian time-warp; Pimmsville on the water. Whereas before the war fifteen stewards sufficed to run the whole thing, now fifty are needed. They may well be almost to a man members of Leander, the rowing club which stands in relation to rowing somewhat as the MCC does to cricket and is, as it were, the third force at Henley. Its pleasant Edwardian clubhouse stands just beside the bridge on the Berkshire side of the Thames and therefore of necessity it stands cheek by jowl with the Regatta. Most of its older members will be there to wave, and of course Leander crews figure prominently on the river; but that does not mean Leander actually *is* the Regatta. The difference is a subtle but important one: while the Regatta accepts no business sponsorship Leander, after a recent palace revolution, does: Jaguar cars have paid a whopping £20,000 just for the benefit of having a marquee at the club for the four days of the Regatta where they can entertain wealthy overseas clients. Pimm's, too, pay substantially to entertain here. Such is the pull of this perennial river party.

Standards are still strictly maintained. Men must wear collars and ties and jackets (although shirt-sleeve order was permitted during the heatwave of 1976) and no woman is admitted to the Stewards' Enclosure in trousers. Within these parameters, however, anything goes, and it is the one occasion in the season when, if anything, the men outdo the women in their gorgeous rainbow striped blazers. The most chic of all male dress at Henley is the pink tie and pink socks which distinguish a Leander member; but really any colours will do and the more garish the better.

The rowing itself may not interest more than a minority,

Above: For the oarsmen at Henley, no exertion can be too much.
Opposite: For the cognoscenti at Henley no magnification can
be too great.

but in fact some two thousand oarsmen from all over the world will be competing. When the Russians first came they could not understand how all the stewards could be English: where was the famous English sense of fair play? It was conveyed to them that Henley stewards are incorruptible and now they race there without a single Russian steward.

Henley is in many ways a racing anomaly. Its length is eccentric – one mile 550 yards, so that to this extent it is out of scale with crews training for Olympic distances. It is also wide enough for only two crews to race at any one time; not several in line abreast as in Olympic racing; and the water they race on is flowing, not still. Nevertheless, because it takes place immediately before the National Rowing Championships of Great Britain at the National Water Sports Centre in Nottingham, it is well worth while for foreign crews to come to Britain for both. Some Americans, for example, regard Henley as the USA's premier regatta, and they usually account for half of all the overseas entries.

They will be racing for a number of highly prized trophies; notably the Grand Challenge Cup, dating from 1839, which has been won by overseas crews thirty times – nine times by Americans, eight times by Russians, six times by Germany, three times by Belgium, and once each by Australia, Switzerland, France, and Bulgaria. In 1986, though, it stayed firmly in British hands when it was won by Nautilus, a code-name for our national squad. Then there is the Ladies Challenge Plate – not, as it might confusingly appear, a trophy ladies compete for, but intended for crews who do not feel they are quite up to Grand standard – and the Thames Challenge Cup, for crews of single college boat clubs, smaller clubs, and schools. The Princess Elizabeth Challenge Club is for schools alone, and was opened to overseas crews in 1964. American and Canadian schools dominated between 1968 and 1981, when they won it twelve times; but recently the GCE exams have made such inroads on the race, at any rate among British schools, that the Special Race for Schools – confined just to the Saturday and Sunday of the Regatta – was instituted in 1974 to get round the problem. You can also see in the specially guarded tent during the Regatta the many trophies given for coxed and coxwainless fours (the idea of doing without a cox

Above: The legendary pink tie of the Leander man.

138

began in 1868 when at the word go F. E. Weatherly, the cox of Brasenose College, Oxford, jumped overboard, allowing his four to win easily); the Silver Goblet for the Pair-Oared Race, and, perhaps most celebrated of all, the Diamond Sculls trophy, instituted in 1850 for single oarsmen.

Henley is hell to get to; for it is quite possible to sit in a traffic jam between the motorway and the town for an hour and a half, a bore that is only alleviated by the sight of pretty girls in the cars ahead of you jumping out to offer champagne to friends in cars behind them. So the answer, as with so many English summer sports, is either to go very early indeed (it would not be a bad idea to arrive at 9 a.m.) or to go by train, or, most stylish of all, to arrive by boat. Provided the weather's kind, and it often is at Henley, there is no more agreeable sight in England than the big launches cruising majestically past, loaded with guests sipping their Pimm's and Veuve Clicquot and listening to the strains of Dixieland jazz from the foredeck. But Henley need not cost you big money; indeed there is nothing to stop you rowing up to the grandstand stretch and tying up on the boom outside it. Provided you don't get in the way you will not be charged or moved.

The real fun of Henley, however, often is to be found slightly behind the scenes. The Regatta service, for instance, is attended even by Russian crews, though curiosity rather than devotion is no doubt their first motive. They will see, if the service runs true to form, at least one clergyman who is a former rowing Blue officiate (the first university boat race in 1829 could boast a future bishop, two deans, and a prebendary on the Oxford boat; two bishops and a dean in the Cambridge boat; and even twenty-five years ago future bishops of Chichester, Gloucester and Lichfield were all rowing Blues); and will hear the stop-watches click as the great sweepstake opens on precisely how many minutes and seconds the sermon will run.

Note too that there is a certain division between the north or Bucks side of Henley and the south or Berkshire side. Official Henley – the Stewards' Enclosure, the Leander club – is south; but a whole new world of near-Henley activities has sprung up on the north side. Here are clubs like Phyllis Court, which, though not officially Henley, have just as good a view

Above: The decorative pink parasol of the Henley punter.

and are just as packed. Here too are the private tents, many taken by firms entertaining clients, on land that has been quietly bought up by the Regatta over the years. The fair has now been moved from the Berkshire bank to a new site up the Wargrave road, following some trouble with its customers.

Like most meticulously run events in the English season, Henley takes an awful lot of hard work behind the scenes. The Chairman of the Regatta is up soon after 5 a.m., patrolling the course to make sure every stick and stone is in place. Car park bookings are painstakingly planned, so that if you ask you can find yourself next to the friends of last year; a thousand boats are stacked so that Russian crews, American crews, Oxford and Cambridge crews are all together.

For the Russians in particular (who have not been recently), Henley proved a culture shock. There have been times when a Soviet crew has arrived at Heathrow in the small hours of the morning and been driven to Christ Church, Oxford, where they have been billeted, and served dawn breakfast by white-coated college staff in what they assume to be a milord's castle. The Russians also attend the draw for the order of races the Saturday before the Regatta, when the Chairman takes a lucky dip from a Henley cup in the town hall. The Russians say they know the draw is fixed; but still can't work out how it's done. It isn't, of course.

In the end, the perennial magic of Henley is its youth. 'Ascot is tired silk,' as Mrs John Garton, wife of the Regatta President summed up; 'Henley is fresh cotton.' Yet paradoxically it was grand old age which starred in one of the most moving spectacles Henley has witnessed in its 150 years: the 1914 Harvard crew rowing over the same course – or part of it – exactly fifty years after it won the Grand Challenge Cup. The odds against them all being there – senators, bankers, surgeons – and able to row were worked out actuarially at 10,000–1. They gave a new Grand Challenge Cup to the Regatta – the old one was so battered it no longer held the proffered Yellow Label champagne – as a tribute to the Leander eight they had beaten in 1914. Gallant fellows, they said, most of whom were destined to die in the war which started a few weeks later.

The best way to be fed and watered at Henley is at a private party in the car park; the scrum inside the Leander tent can be hot and tiring, and it can take you a good half-hour in the queue before you get served. Best of all, of course, is to get an invitation to stay locally. Many local wives with large houses put up visiting crews from abroad and make useful income out of it despite the gargantuan appetites of these young giants. One oddity of Henley is that the whole blue-and-white extravaganza is temporary: the marquees come down after the Regatta; but not quite so quickly as they once did. It was a brainwave to decide to hold a festival of music and art immediately afterwards, utilizing all these pavilions of pleasure; and there can surely be no experience quite like sitting on a grandstand sipping the Widow, while in front of you on a floating stage a great London orchestra regales you with a Mozart concerto. Punts and cruisers tie up to eavesdrop on the Horn Concerto No. 4 with that lovely dancing movement as a gibbous moon gently prevails over a salmon sunset and skiffs skim silently over the silver river. It is about as near as any of us will get to Sydney Smith's celebrated definition of heaven – eating *pâté de foie gras* to the sound of trumpets.

Yet let no one believe that heaven at Henley is only for music-lovers. 'I spent happy hours on the Isis, but the best was Henley,' declared the writer Nigel Nicolson. 'There we were in competition with the finest crews of several nationalities, and at no moment in my life have I experienced so *sustained* a wish to excel. For those few days we lived in dread of the next race, discussing tactics, grooming the boat, eating enormously, sleeping long – and then the last terrified backward glance at the course before the race began in distant privacy to end ten minutes later between banks of parasols and tumultuous acclaim. Those were ecstatic moments.'

Christopher Dodd, elegant historian of Henley Royal Regatta, says it has always been a showcase of English rowing. 'Until the Second World War it was a bastion of the sort of amateurism which put people who worked with their hands beyond the pale, but now it encompasses most aspects of British rowing. Since the turn of the century it has been a major battlefield between the English and foreigners, particularly Americans. It keeps its own oligarchical counsel and its own rules but cautiously keeps up with change in sport, and thrives.

All pals together at the pavilion of pleasure.

Even at Henley you may have to sit one out.

Everybody loves Henley even if they hate it, and if, like Nigel Nicolson, you get the added pleasure of earning a place there with a crew, and experience there the elusive ecstasy which all oarsmen seek, then you have found heaven on earth.'

How to get in

Payment of £3 on the day will gain entrance to the Regatta Enclosure, which corresponds roughly to the Tattersalls area on a racecourse. For the more elegant Stewards' Enclosure, entry is not so easy – the 4,500 members pay £50 a year which entitles them to a metal badge for entry on each day and the right to purchase guests' badges. Anyone can apply to join but you must be proposed and seconded by a member, and naturally preference is given to those with rowing experience.

Despite the fact that the Regatta never advertises, it is becoming increasingly popular, and guests' badges are much in demand for the two most 'social' days, Saturday and Sunday, for which there are 7,500 guests' badges available. Therefore an early approach to a member to buy badges on your behalf is necessary. If you don't know a member, the secretary, Mr Richard Goddard, can help by suggesting the names of members who live in your area. For those not taking picnics, the Stewards' Enclosure has a luncheon tent for which tickets (lunch £10.60, tea £3.40) can be ordered in advance or on the day. Guest badge prices are: Wednesday £6; Thursday £8; Friday £14; Saturday £17; Sunday £13.

How to get there

Henley-on-Thames is in Oxfordshire and is thirty-six miles from London. It can be reached by following the M4 motorway, but be prepared for slow going (unless you're a very early bird) once you join the A423 near Maidenhead. Trains to Henley run from Paddington Station and coaches from Victoria Coach Station. Car park tickets can be ordered from the Regatta Office in advance or purchased on the day at the following prices: Wednesday £4; Thursday £5; and £7 each for Friday, Saturday and Sunday.

Note: Those who think they would enjoy the Henley Festival can write for the mailing list to the Henley Festival office at 103-109, Wardour Street, London W1V 3TD or telephone them at 01-437 9711. Their box office opens at Henley itself in the first week of April. Telephone: 0491 575751 but postal bookings still at the London address.

COWES REGATTA
AUGUST

owes is probably best at dusk; the lights of the destroyers riding in the harbour spring on and the launches ply between the big yachts and the jetty, bringing guests ashore for the round of cocktail parties and dances. It is almost as if some of the characters from a Noël Coward naval comedy had wandered into a painting by Fragonard.

Most keenly awaited of all is the launch bringing the Duke of Edinburgh ashore from the Royal Yacht *Britannia*. She flies through the water at impressive speed and looks as if she must crash against the quayside. Miraculously, however, she seems to slam on some sort of marine disc brakes at the last moment and pulls up at exactly the right spot. The immaculate *Britannia* sailors go through the boathook drill with majestic precision, even at these breathtaking speeds. The Duke leaps ashore – lean, energetic and purposeful – and disappears into the Royal Yacht Squadron of which he is Admiral.

It is one of the most exclusive clubs in the world. It was formed in 1815 by forty-two gentlemen who said they were 'interested in the sailing of yachts in salt water'. The entrance fee was then three guineas and the annual subscription two guineas. Today the three hundred full members pay £300 a year for the privilege of belonging. There are also 150 naval members who must be Commanders or above. The membership list is studded with establishment names: Edward Heath and Edward du Cann; Lord Brabazon and Sir Owen Aisher. Lord Camrose is a trustee and, until his recent death, Sir Max Aitken was a colourful member. The blackball is still used there; but more often because applicants are not really interested in yachting than for more social reasons.

Members of the Squadron have no fewer than three uniforms. There is the undress uniform – a blue reefer (blazer, to you and me) with black buttons showing the Royal Yacht Squadron cypher; for more formal wear there is an extra smart reefer with silver buttons; and then, for very grand occasions, there is a mess jacket with black facings, dark blue waistcoat and trousers.

Though the Squadron does not have the control over sailing that the Jockey Club does over racing, there are certain broad similarities. The RYS has an institutional role in Cowes yachting. During the Regatta, the races are run each day from

Right: The Royal Yacht Squadron – nerve centre of Cowes Regatta, where all the races are started.

the deck of the Squadron by whichever club is in charge that day – Royal London, Royal Corinthian, or Royal Southern. The committees of these guest clubs will be invited to set the course and use the facilities, but the Squadron servant will fire the gun at their say-so.

The position of women at the Squadron remains ambiguous. They are admitted, but only on certain days and at certain hours and in certain parts of the club. Many members of the Squadron, though, will have a house on the island still; for example, Harriet Brabazon, wife of the young Lord Brabazon, spent some six weeks on the island in 1985 while waiting for her second child and with a nanny to help look after the first. Others rent houses for the season in Bembridge at weekly rentals which range from £250 to £5,000 a week. One such tenant in 1985 was heard vowing privately to make sure the Inland Revenue knew about the vast rent he had paid for his house. The Squadron itself, incidentally, is no slouch at making money either; its policy in investing shrewdly in port and fine wines over many years has meant that it has not only had some excellent drinking, but also a handsome capital appreciation on those wines it later sells off.

The key social event is the Squadron dance on Monday night, when the festivities go on into the small hours. Democracy has not yet percolated through there, and even in the summer of 1985 it was possible to work below stairs for a thrifty £1.10 per hour.

Nevertheless, and against all the odds, knowledgeable sailing men have noticed a slight but perceptible loosening-up at the Squadron in the last twelve to eighteen months. Where it stems from is not clear. It might even be a function of the new populist mode filtering down from the Palace through Prince Philip. Whatever the explanation, recently soaking wet yachtsmen have been allowed to drink on the deck – the area from which the races are controlled – where there is not exactly a bar but drinks and a cash box. The prices, however, are far from populist – £3 for a glass of Pimm's, for example. It is another quaint custom at the Squadron that no drinks are dispensed as singles – only doubles or multiples.

If, however, you are still not *persona grata* at the Squadron, there are far more relaxed places to go. The unlegislated social focus of Cowes is the Groves and Gutteridge marina, where crews gather in late afternoon or early evening at the beer, wine or champagne bars to talk over the day's sailing before going on to other parties. Or they can stay at the marina and dine at the Fastnet, the new restaurant there. And then there are all the other yachting clubs to try.

The Royal Corinthian Yacht Club, for instance, is right next door to the Royal Yacht Squadron on Castle Rock. It actually overlooks the Squadron beneath it and was once owned by Rosa Lewis, the legendary lady who ran the raffish Cavendish Hotel in Jermyn Street and won the favour of so many aristocrats from King Edward VII down. When Castle Rock came on the market in 1925 the Royal Yacht Squadron were intending to buy it as a ladies' annexe, but Rosa Lewis kept on outbidding them until they dropped out. The balls she threw there between the wars in the little annexe at the bottom of her garden outshone anything the Squadron could do. Rosa, alas, is long gone; but the Corinthians who took over run it as a fairly relaxed but still elegant club where a collar and tie are still required after 8 p.m. Even before 8, when you can leave your tie off, if you know the ropes, you never wear it *outside* your blazer; such are the fine nuances on which Cowes society is based.

There are a number of other such nuances. One is that this is strictly called the Royal Corinthian *at Cowes*. The RC itself is at Burnham; though its Cowes outpost is open all the year and you can stay there for the night or the weekend if you belong. The membership covers a wide spectrum: from the classic old duffers, through the wily yachtsmen still driving day-boats that have seen much service, to the well-heeled young. It is a well-managed club that makes money by issuing temporary badges in Cowes week; and it is the only club to have a yacht named after it: the Corinthian One-size 28-foot open day boat. It costs £100 to join and the subscription is £50 a year.

Further down the little quayside comes the Royal London Yacht Club, which will cost you £150 a year; but most democratic of all is the Island Sailing Club, costing a mere £40 a year, to which anyone interested in sailing can get temporary membership in Cowes week. The atmosphere there is free and easy, despite the bouncers on the door recruited from the

An old Thames barge meets a modern Maxi racing yacht.

The Groves and Gutteridge yard at Cowes – unlegislated social centre of the Regatta.

warders of Parkhurst Prison, and, incidentally, the Duke himself has been seen having a quiet beer there like everybody else.

One warning about Cowes: while the utmost duffer can usually tell who has won the Derby or whacked in a goal at polo, there is no such simplicity about sailing. Anyone standing on the quayside will merely see a rather pretty but totally confusing flurry of scudding sails amid the spray. The only way to enjoy the racing properly is to go on board, as I had the luck to do one year with Mr Tony Boyden and his *Flica II*. Even though there was twenty-one tons of lead in her hull for stability, he was a little worried about my weight, but relented and lent me a pale blue sweater and yachting cap so that I didn't look too out of place. Boyden himself was at the helm, assisted by a tactician-navigator, a sailmaster and a crew of eight.

My main concern was not to fall overboard. Boyden explained that nowadays he had to stop for anyone who did; in the old days they had to fend for themselves. Our first few minutes were extremely confusing. As we tacked up to the first mark, and the cry of 'Ready About' was raised, I found myself lying flat on my stomach amidships one moment, then scrambling over to fall flat on the other side of the boat as the crew, in a frenzy of energy, set the sails for our new tack. They pride themselves on tacking in seventeen seconds. When we came downwind I saw the gay spinnaker in action for the first time – a large, ballooning sail designed to catch the largest amount of wind.

Many of the tactics were lost on me. I gathered that you have to 'tweak' the spinnaker every so often to stop it collapsing; I soon learned what the crew member up in the bows meant by 'pinching'; he was warning us that we were trying to sail too close into the wind. I couldn't help reflecting how much of ordinary English idiom derives from sailing. But I never understood exactly why we took down the spinnaker when we did and ran up the genoa (a twelve-metre yacht's equivalent to a jib – if you know what a jib is) in its place.

Nor did I ever gather the exact significance of the little extra sail called the staysail, which we sometimes employed and at other times pulled in again. I do know that it was most exciting racing and that on the final leg we just lay flat and

*Not with a whimper but a bang – fireworks burst over Marine
Parade to round off the racing.*

crossed our fingers, hoping that some extra puff of wind would drive us over the finish first. But we had no such luck. We had been sailing for five hours, and at the end of that time there were only five minutes spanning the first three boats. Then there was time for a leisurely bath ashore before changing for the Royal Yacht Squadron dance in the evening.

Sailing like this, while not quite as pricey as polo, is hardly cheap. The X-boat class, first designed in 1893, and thus a very old-fashioned open day boat, fielded no fewer than seventy-four starters at the 1986 Regatta. It will cost you from £2,000 to £5,000 to buy and £1,000 a year to run – roughly the same as a medium-sized car. A Dragon class yacht will cost £8,000 second-hand and £12,000 to £14,000 new; about £2,000 a year to run. A quarter-tonner will set you back £25,000, a half tonner £50,000 to £80,000, and a one-ton yacht (the minimum size for the Admiral's Cup) will cost £200,000 to £300,000 and £20,000 a year to run. Still, you can go racing with social *cachet* for £5,000 down and £1,000 a year.

Yet since there is no longer enough private money to finance all the boats, sponsorship has come to Cowes as elsewhere. The dynamic furniture chain, Sandhurst, now underwrite Cowes week and Mumm Champagne sponsor the Admiral's Cup. But it is really the foreign ships and foreign money that give Cowes its unique style, and the best party of the week is said to be the one given by Ozcrew, the collective name for the fraternity of Australian crew men who are now such a boisterous and indispensable part of Cowes. In its style it's about as far from the Royal Yacht Squadron as the human mind can envisage. At Cowes, in fact, if you know your way around, anything goes.

How to get there

The best way to arrive is on your own boat. To take a car to the Island in high summer without booking is more difficult than entry to the Royal Yacht Squadron. British Rail Seaspeed Hovercraft and the Red Funnel Hydrofoil take twenty minutes from Southampton. The latter is quieter and more comfortable. Booking is essential at peak times. For those who have more time, Red Funnel also run a car ferry, which takes foot passengers as well; the voyage takes forty minutes. Car ferries run from Lymington to Yarmouth in the west and from Portsmouth to Fishbourne in the east. Bookings are accepted from October onward for the following year, and July and August Saturday places are usually all gone by January. Mid-week reservations are easier but the car space should be reserved two or three weeks before sailing. It may be important to get back too, so the return booking must be remembered as well.

CROQUET AT HURLINGHAM

AUGUST/SEPTEMBER

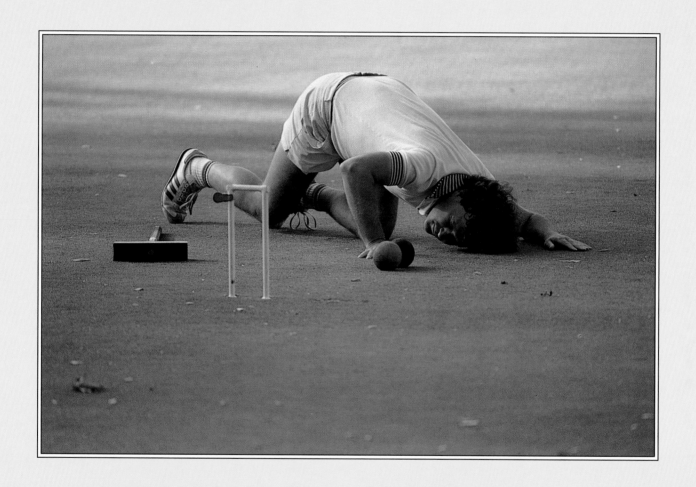

No one knows for certain where croquet comes from; though curiously enough its origins are almost certainly not French. It has variously been claimed that it started in India, Switzerland, Mauritius and even China. Most theories have in common, though, the notion that it was played in some elementary form in Ireland before it was introduced to England. It was played there perhaps as early as the 1830s and was brought to England by some person or persons unknown about 1851.

By 1864 John Jaques of Hatton Garden, then the only serious maker of croquet equipment in England, issued the first comprehensive code of laws, a copy of which was included with each set he sold. Three years later 65,000 copies had been printed. 'The game was becoming popular,' comments Lt.-Col. D.M.C. Prichard in *The History of Croquet*. 'At first it was the ladies who were the keenest. It was a novel experience for them to be able to take part in a game in the open air, particularly in the company of men. Soon the young men saw its good points, too, and began to play for pleasure rather than just to oblige. These were the days of tight chaperonage as well as tight croquet (which meant placing one foot firmly on one's own ball and croqueting the other as far away as possible). There was sometimes an ulterior motive, apart from the tactical advantage of hitting one's opponent off into the bushes: if the opponent was an attractive young lady, it enabled the young man gallantly to assist her in the search, concealed in a friendly shrubbery from the eagle eyes of the ever vigilant chaperones.'

The received opinion of croquet – that it was a diversion for curates and spinsters in crinolines on rectory lawns – endured for more than a century. It is indeed only in recent times that the game has been perceived as requiring a unique blend of intellectual and physical skills – a cross between snooker and chess played on grass. A croquet break can last as long as half an hour, and some close fought games last three hours. Nor is there ever any need to concede defeat at croquet. Some of the most exciting games have been won when a player who has not yet scored wrests the initiative from an opponent who has made 24 or 25 of the 26 points you need to win. It needs forward planning, accuracy, skill and mental agility. It remains, all the same, one of the few truly sportsmanlike and genuinely amateur games.

The governing body of British – and indeed world – croquet is the Croquet Association, run by its secretary, Mr Brian Macmillan, from an office inside the Hurlingham Club on the Thames near Putney Bridge. There are about ten thousand people playing croquet in Britain, says Mr Macmillan, of whom some four thousand play competitively. The sport is now booming; in the first eight weeks of 1986 he enrolled eight new clubs. The two greatest events in the croquet calendar are the Open Championships in August, when the best forty-eight players compete under a handicap system, and the President's Cup in September, perhaps the apogee of the season, for here only the best eight players are in contention. Despite the old crinoline image, and the fact that in the country at large the male-female ratio is roughly six to four, in top competitive croquet women have yet to reach anything like parity; only two women competed in the Open and neither got further than the second round; and there were none at all in the President's Cup.

The top croquet player in Britain at present is unquestionably Nigel Aspinall, a young man of independent means; his nearest contender is a merchant banker, Steve Mulliner. The thirties are held to be the best decade for top croquet but there are some promising young players in their early twenties and

*Above: Long shadows on manicured lawns: the langorous
pleasure of croquet at Hurlingham*

The music which accompanies this civilized sport.

teens. In the summer of 1986, Hurlingham, the Lord's of croquet, was again host to the three-sided Test between Australia, New Zealand and Britain. Britain won the previous series at almost the last hoop; this time, however, New Zealand prevailed, and more comfortably, winning five matches to Great Britain's three and Australia's one. The intelligent game (as it has been dubbed, to the embarrassment of the Croquet Association, who want everybody to feel able to play) is now played in most European countries except Germany; in South Africa it is very strong, although in accordance with the Gleneagles agreement, the CA does not arrange fixtures there; they play it in India and Pakistan, Egypt and Greece; Japan started two years ago and already has eight clubs. To the gratification of the CA, the Japanese have taken up the British croquet game, not the American (in which the essential difference is that the ball goes dead when it has gone through the hoop).

Croquet is fortunate to have Hurlingham as its head-quarters; it is, as Lord Hatherton remarked in 1835, 'one of the most delightful villas I have ever entered on the banks of the Thames', and in its forty acres of land six thousand members (many from the diplomatic corps) can enjoy a wide range of games: tennis, golf, cricket, bowling, and squash as well as croquet. It costs £304.75 a year to belong to the Hurlingham; but just along the river at Parson's Green you can play croquet for £12 a year. The only piece of equipment you need is a mallet costing some £40; the game for curates and crinolined spinsters has become everyman's.

How to get there
Hurlingham can be reached by Tube on the Wimbledon line to Putney Bridge Station, from where it is five minutes' walk. Buses 39, 80, 85, 93, 264 and 265 go to Putney Bridge Station; numbers 14, 22, and 30 go to Putney Bridge itself.

How to get in
Write or phone Mr Brian Macmillan, administrative secretary of The Croquet Association, at Hurlingham Club, Ranelagh Gardens, London SW6 3PR (tel. 01 736 3148).

THE LAST NIGHT OF THE PROMS

SEPTEMBER

Proms were literally concerts where the audience could walk about, but now where they stand, if they so choose, to hear good music at bargain prices. Although the first English promenade concerts were held as early as 1838, the word now instantly conveys to every Englishman the great summer season at the Royal Albert Hall; an eight-week feast of music which culminates in the Dionysiac ritual of the Last Night. Two hundred million television viewers tune in to see the shenanigans as the promenaders – some of whom have been queuing for several days to get in – sing all the grand old chauvinist tunes: the over-worked 'Land of Hope and Glory', the shameless 'Rule Britannia', and the quasi-mystical 'Jerusalem'. From the boxes above, the scene is a weird amalgam of chaos and order. Within the oval shell that houses the promenaders there is a forest of Union Jacks and patriotic straw hats bobbing to the beat of the music; but the promenaders know very well that they are part of the performance and will not fail to deck the bust of Sir Henry Wood, founder of the modern prom, with his evergreen laurel wreath in time for the cameras to record their tribute. The BBC cameraman down among the promenaders is both comrade and commander, now lifting his movable trolley high over their heads to get a panning shot, now sinking down to hobnob among them in a matey populist mode.

The entire event is indeed most carefully orchestrated, designed and choreographed. The massed choirs of the BBC Singers and BBC Symphony Chorus provide a kaleidoscopic backdrop, the men creating a penguin effect with their rows of white shirts and black ties and dinner jackets, the women a great splash of colour in their rainbow of evening dresses; a myriad of colours, but only one colour to each dress. The thunder of the giant organ lends an almost dreamlike quality to the occasion when it comes in for 'Jerusalem'; and the hallucinogenic echo is struck again by the rows of baffles hanging from the roof like so many giant inverted mushrooms. Another BBC cameraman in pink ear muffs swings right to capture the banked choristers, thus underlining again that sense of being in some drug-induced trance. Yet all is familiar and safe. The ample-bosomed contralto, Sarah Walker, is there as earth-mother to lead us into 'Rule Britannia': 'When Britain first at Heaven's command / Arose from out the azure main.' Then on to the chorus, at which the whole vast concourse, including the well-heeled people up in the boxes, primed on bubbly and canapés, rises to its feet in an orgy of patriotic frenzy: 'Britons never, never, never / Shall be slaves.'

Actually you don't have to be a Brit to join in the fun. At the 1985 Last Night the first half had Gershwin's Piano Concerto to act as sandwich piece between Holst's Fugal Overture and Walton's Gloria, with Shura Cherkassky, the American Romantic pianist, to give us an authentically jazz-tinged account of Gershwin's quintessentially American score. Then the second half opened with Sousa's block-busting 'Stars and Stripes Forever', and one couldn't help noting a few brave Stars and Stripes waving amid the battalions of Union Jacks.

Vernon Handley, conducting, did not offer the glamour-boy image of a Malcolm Sargent or the youthful prodigy effect created by a Simon Rattle; however, he did jolly the promenaders into facing the fact that their singing was not all that it might be; and it wasn't just his judgement; he'd had letters from viewers in Sweden to say that if the promenaders couldn't sing better than that, *they'd* come and do it for them. So what about a little practice on 'Wider still and wider / Be thy boundaries set'? Disgraceful sentiments, of course, but at least, he suggested, let's get the beat right. The promenaders good-

*Above: the apogee of patriotism – promenaders applaud and the
Union Jack is flaunted.*
*Opposite: The melodies may change, but the promenaders go on
for ever.*

159

naturedly practised in a kind of plain-chant and, indeed, did seem to get it rather more right when the orchestra led them into the piece itself.

Simple emotions are never far below the surface at the Last Night; and the elderly chorister who took a solo bow to mark his retirement after singing with that great choir for a solid half-century drew a spontaneous rendering of 'For He's a Jolly Good Fellow', and not a few tears. It was all, in fact, good harmless fun; but let us not altogether forget that this is the end of a celebration of music which, in its scale and variety, has no equal in the world. It all began in 1895, in a typically eccentric English way, when a music-lover and throat specialist called George Clark Cathcart gave £2,000 for a new series of Proms at the old Queen's Hall; on condition that the existing high pitch, ruinous to singers' voices (he held) be abandoned in favour of the lower French pitch.

Wood accepted the challenge. He was a tireless champion of modern music who played the work of Tchaikovsky, Sibelius, Scriabin and Debussy to English audiences before they were widely known, conducted the first performances in England of Mahler's First, Fourth, Seventh, and Eighth Symphonies, and introduced the music of Janáček to the English. Every major English composer of his lifetime was performed at the Proms; and still is. All this in the capital of what one German once called the land without music.

How to get in
The Royal Albert Hall seats 5,600 people, but on the Last Night of the Proms many more people are packed into every last bit of standing room as well. The Box Office rule is that people have to go to four other concerts in the Proms season (July to September) before they can apply for two tickets to the Last Night. A season ticket for a seat in the arena costs £50 and a gallery seat is £36; for a half-season ticket the prices are £32.50 (arena) and £22 (gallery). Season tickets allow entry on the Last Night. Bookings should be made well in advance to the Box Office, the Henry Wood Promenade Concerts, the Royal Albert Hall, Kensington, London SW7 (tel. 01 589 8212). A programme of the concerts is published each May and is widely available at newsagents or from the Albert Hall.

How to get there
The Albert Hall is in a road called Kensington Gore, on the south side of Hyde Park, almost opposite Kensington Palace. Car parking spaces are very limited on the Last Night and it is best to travel by taxi or Underground – the Hall is five-or-so minutes' walk from South Kensington station. The buses which pass the door are nos. 52, 73 and 9.

Previous page: Wider still and wider, be thy boundaries set . . .
and on the Last Night of the Proms, nobody disagrees.

PHEASANT SHOOTING

OCTOBER/NOVEMBER

It's 9.15 in the morning at Burley, the enormous house just outside Oakham owned by Joss Hanbury. However, his passion is fox hunting and he leaves the shooting over his two thousand acre estate to his friend and neighbour, Norman MacRoberts, who farms five miles away. Norman has been running the shoot for five years now; this is the last time they will meet this season, except for the beaters' shoot when tenant farmers and anybody else who should be thanked join the beaters in a final day's shooting. Today, though, he has arranged for six friends to spend the day with him so there will be seven guns going out instead of the more normal eight. They haven't arrived yet, but the beaters are already assembling in a line outside the house with the Ford truck that will carry them around the estate; each holds a long stake with which he will beat the undergrowth to set the pheasants flying, and many of them have their own dogs to help them.

The gamekeeper, Alec, a cheery ruddy-faced fellow, tells me that he reared nine hundred pheasants for this season of which five hundred have already been shot. Today he and the beaters will have a sweepstake on the bag, but he is hoping for seventy or eighty. Of course, as he tells me, it gets harder as the season goes on. The pheasant get craftier. 'The other day I found one sitting in a rabbit hole and we had to get the dog to get him out.' Already there are fourteen beaters and six dogs, and there are two ladies who will act as professional pickers-up of the game, in all our party numbering twenty-four.

Soon the guns (the friends who will be doing the actual shooting) arrive and Norman MacRoberts asks them to draw for their positions. This is a device which saves the host from the blame if one of his guests has a poor day's shooting. There is a theory that being in the middle of the line of guns provides better sport; the draw ensures that you will always have the same neighbour but change position at each drive – that is to say, at each point where the shoot will take place.

On many shoots there are eight drives and they stop for lunch in the middle. Here at Oakham, however, they go straight through till 3 p.m., then have a convivial lunch to discuss the day's sport over some good wine. This can go on till 7 p.m. and has been known to go on till 9. But the serious business has to be tackled first.

I set off with Norman in his four-wheel-drive Subaru for the first drive, which was right on the top of the estate. As we bumped over the muddy tracks he explained that at Oakham they only shoot cock pheasant, whereas it is more normal to shoot both cocks and hens. Since Alec only spends half of his time keeping and the other half as woodman, they don't rear their own pheasant but buy them in at six weeks old and can therefore choose to buy cocks only. 'If you only shoot cocks,' Norman explains, 'the hens are wild. A reared hen is no good. They just don't have the same blood as a wild hen.' I asked him about the guns they use; he said most people that day would be using English Holland & Holland guns, made in London. He said the Spanish and Italians make good guns but he knew little about them. It later transpired, though, that a good gun would cost between £12,000 and £14,000.

We arrived at our first drive, a wooded area on the edge of the estate where Norman was not hoping for much luck. He would have preferred eight guns; each of the drives has eight pegs, and it is his job to plan where they shall be. With one gun missing he has to decide which peg will be vacant. The actual quality of the marksmanship will also dictate to some extent whether or not the pegs are moved closer to the wood. 'We get some people here who never hit a bloody thing, so they put the pegs fifteen yards nearer.' Today, though, the pegs stay in their normal positions. I asked him what would be the best weather for shooting. 'Like today,' he said, 'a light breeze and dry. They don't fly well if there is too much moisture in the air.'

The guns took up their positions, the two lady pickers-up stood some two hundred yards back and the beaters, who had disappeared behind the wood, could be heard slowly coming towards us rattling their sticks through the copse and emitting a series of strange warbling sounds. At first nothing happened, and then the first pheasant came winging high through the air, plump, golden and beautiful. The guns opened up and suddenly its wings ceased to beat. Then it curved down in a long arc to the ground. Then one or two more came whizzing straight towards us at no more than head height going very fast; but not too fast for Norman and his friends who nailed them as they went by. Soon the air was filled with fluttering feathers and the acrid smell of gunpowder. They had shot eight pheasant,

Above: The essential accessories of a good day's shooting: the flagman (above) and the beaters (below).

165

somewhat better than Norman had expected. 'We found some cartridges in the wood,' Norman explained, 'which means there have been some poachers. It isn't so much that they have been shooting, but the disturbance can drive the pheasant away.' They had also seen a lot of wild hens flying in that drive, which he considered a good augury for next year.

We went on to the next drive, and I stood next to another gun who told me that he too farmed nearby; though it seemed to be a fairly upmarket kind of farming because he lived at Rockingham Castle. Again the pheasant sizzled between us, going fast, but the guns opened up simultaneously and they fell. My neighbour told me they prefer the birds to fly higher because it provides better sport. Indeed there is a basic difference in attitude between the gamekeeper, who is interested in how many birds they kill, and the guns, who are more interested in how good the sport was.

I thought we had done well, but Norman said that over the hedge one of the guns had missed four birds out of five. I asked if they often only winged the bird rather than killing it outright. He said it happened occasionally if the guns were shooting badly, but it seemed that day most of them were killed stone dead. A few fluttered for some minutes on the ground but then that was that. I asked Norman how you learn to shoot. He said that clay pigeon shooting was the only way. And how long would it take to become a decent shot? About a year, he thought. And how many times would a good gun expect to hit his pheasant? He thought seventy-five to eighty per cent of the time – maybe more. But the proportion of cartridges to kill would be lower, because you sometimes took a shot at someone else's bird or at a stupid pigeon.

I asked him about the beaters: was it skilled work? Not really, but those who brought dogs had to have the skill to control them. A good beater must go *through* the rough ground where the pheasant hide, not round it. Most of them were local chaps who had taken a day off their jobs and would be paid £10 for their efforts.

We were at our third drive, this time a kale field with the beaters going through it towards where I stood and four guns in a line to our right to intercept the birds as they flew out. Again, that strange trilling and banging sound as they emerged from

The bag at Burley after a good day's shooting – and tonight they will sleep well.

the undergrowth, but few pheasant this time, although one almost overhead fell vertically at our feet.

Next came a drive which Norman said was probably almost unique, where the guns walked in single file down a long ride with four hundred acres of woodland on their right, into which the birds headed from along a ten-acre strip of woodland. It makes for good sport because the trees are high and the pheasant fly over them, providing a good target. Spirits seemed to rise as these beautiful birds fell in a hail of hot lead. So we went on towards the fifth drive. Norman explained that he looked after three of the woods on the estate himself. He liked to be up early in the morning and see a lot of pheasant, even though a fortnight later when he went shooting they would be gone. He had been out forty-one days this season, but last year had been ridiculous – he had had fifty organized days' shooting; but he explained that as an arable farmer he has almost nothing to do at this time of year. It is a short season which opens on the first week of October (though at Burley they do not start until the third week of November), and goes on through December and January.

It was now around noon and we had been on the move for nearly four hours. It was time to stop and take out their silver flasks and have a swill of sloe gin. Norman's cousin, Corker, had also taken the precaution of bringing along some potted shrimps to stave off hunger until the late lunch. While we sat and discussed the shoot, our faithful beaters were on their way to the fifth drive. And here, Corker asked me to stand – or rather sit on my shooting stick – as near as I could to him. He said that accidents were very rare in England but you never knew what could happen in the heat of battle, and the nearer I sat the safer I would be. He added thoughtfully that Americans who came over for the grouse shooting were famous for accidentally shooting each other.

He said that there was undoubtedly quite a lot of poaching: 'No one resents the good village poacher who gets a couple for his pot. They are very clever and know when the keeper is in the pub. But the professional poacher is a different matter altogether.'

The sixth drive was through a copse, and then, for the seventh and last drive of the day, we drove right to the other side of the estate and down a long ride with the house looming upon us. It was probably the best sport of all, with the pheasant flying high and with both dogs and beaters busily engaged foraging in the woods for those that had fallen out of sight. After a good day's shooting, Norman remarked as we drove back, you sleep well.

Where
Unlike grouse shooting, pheasant shooting takes place nationwide, on estates small and large from Cornwall to Scotland. There are a number of commercial agencies (including some of the larger London estate agents such as Humberts, tel. 01 629 6700, and Strutt and Parker, tel. 01 629 7282) which organize places with syndicates for a day or for a season. The minimum charge for being placed on a shoot is around £200 a day, depending on the quality of the shoot.

Anyone wishing to shoot in Great Britain first has to contact the local police station for a shotgun certificate (£12), and for pheasant shooting a game licence is necessary (£6 a year from main post offices).

Further information can be obtained from The British Association for Shooting and Conservation, Marford Hill, Rossett, Clwyd LL12 0HL (tel. 0244 570881).

There are two good magazines associated with the sport: The Shooting Times *(weekly) at 10 Sheet Street, Windsor, Berkshire (tel. 0735 56061) and* The Shooting Life *(quarterly) at Weir Bank, Bray-on-Thames, Maidenhead, Berkshire (tel. 073583 668).*

When
The Pheasant shooting begins on 1 October each year and ends on 1 February. It is against the law to shoot pheasant outside these dates.

FOX HUNTING

NOVEMBER/DECEMBER

'It is difficult to decide,' wrote Barry Campbell in *The Badminton Tradition*, 'whether fox hunting was invented for the benefit of the Dukes of Beaufort, or whether the Dukes of Beaufort were invented to hunt the fox.' Well said; for Badminton, seat of the Dukes of Beaufort, has some claim to be the unlegislated capital of fox hunting, and the grand old 10th Duke, Master of the Beaufort Hunt from 1924 till his death in 1984, appears in the *Guinness Book of Records* as the man who spent more days in the saddle hunting – some ten years of his life – than any other. There is a pleasant fable that fox hunting began at Badminton when Henry, 5th Duke of Beaufort (1744-1803) returning one day to Badminton after a disappointing day's stag hunting, threw his hounds into Silk Wood, where they found a fox which gave them such a good run that thereafter the Duke decided to hunt the fox exclusively.

Something like that may well have happened; but in fact the fox has been hunted in one form or another since medieval times and something like modern fox hunting could be discerned in the north of England late in the sixteenth century. 'It is in Yorkshire,' as Raymond Carr tells us in *English Fox Hunting*, 'that we find the first example of what would come to be the classic fusion of a great landed aristocrat and his tenant farmers in a common enthusiasm for fox hunting. The "wicked" Duke of Buckingham – he seduced Lady Shrewsbury, and then shot her husband in a duel – retired from the court of Charles II and spent most of his time fox hunting and died in 1687 of a chill caught while watching a fox dug out. Whatever his reputation in the south, in the north Buckingham was a mighty MFH and "our duke" stories about him were still current among farmers in the 1890s.'

England had many built-in advantages to make it the perfect hunting country. Enclosure of the land meant more fences and provided many more natural obstacles for riders to jump over. By 1800 English horses were the best in the world, and the English thoroughbred the perfect hunter. English hounds were equally pre-eminent. 'In thee alone, fair land of liberty, is bred the perfect hound,' wrote Peter Beckford in 1779, the first English writer to chronicle fox hunting both accurately and elegantly. All well-bred English foxhounds, indeed, go back in direct 'tail male' to five hounds bred between

1748 and 1900. Yet not only were English horses and hounds the best in the world; such brilliant originals as Hugo Meynell, Master of the Quorn, the great midlands hunt, from 1753 to 1800, brought to fox hunting a sophistication and subtlety which had previously been absent.

Meynell was a hound breeder; he sought to produce 'fine noses and stout running; a combination of strength and beauty, and steadiness with high mettle'; qualities which are just as much valued in the hunting field two hundred years on. Having bred the hounds so lovingly, he hunted them with a finesse not previously seen. The huntsman became for the first time the central figure in the hunt and his skills essential to the success of the day. 'Hounds hunt hares themselves,' as Raymond Carr remarks; 'they have to be made to work for foxes. Left alone they will not run but only potter about. The whole importance of Meynell's system is revealed in the time of his meets; he did not hunt full-bellied foxes at crack of dawn, but in mid-morning when they could be expected to run.' The Hampshire yeoman farmers disapproved of these mid-morning meets: 'We took care to be at the covert side before dawn,' wrote one; 'we killed our fox early and had a good long afternoon for drinking.' Still, it was the mid-morning meet that prevailed; the Beaufort, for example, now normally meets at 10.45 a.m.; the Vale of the White Horse next door at 11.

'It is very strange, and very melancholy,' said Dr Johnson, 'that the paucity of human pleasures should ever persuade us to call hunting one of them.' On the whole fox hunting has had a bad press from English writers, though it was an Irishman, Oscar Wilde, who encapsulated the case against the sport most neatly in his celebrated epigram: 'The English country gentleman galloping after a fox – the unspeakable in full pursuit of the uneatable.' Yet Peter Beckford, said a contemporary, 'would bag a fox in Greek, find a hare in Latin, inspect his kennels in Italian, and direct the economy of his stables in exquisite French.' While no one would accuse Robert Smith Surtees of fastidiousness, his enormous zest and *joie-de-vivre* in the hunting field have appealed to many with no aspirations ever to ride to hounds, and his epitaph on the sport will take some beating: ' 'Unting is all that's worth living for – all time is lost wot is not spent in 'unting – it is like the hair we breathe – if

*Above: The Beaufort Hunt hounds, one of the finest packs in
England, set out from Badminton.*

we have it not we die – it's the sport of kings, the image of war without its guilt, and only five-and-twenty per cent of its danger.' He also encapsulated that odd ambivalence of the hunting man towards his quarry: 'It ar'n't that I loves the fox less, but that I loves the 'ound more.'

This curious respect for the wily fox as an opponent worthy to pit one's wits against is echoed in all the sagas of Reynard the Fox from Aesop to Caxton and from Geoffrey Chaucer to John Masefield; you can hear it again in the profile of the 10th Duke of Beaufort by his old friend, the late Sir Peter Farquhar, former Master of the Portman (among other packs) and one of the greatest authorities on hound breeding: 'We were fishing together in Ireland on the river Slaney. The beat we were fishing was owned by a friend whose foxhounds were kennelled a few hundred yards from the river. Before starting out that morning, Master (a nickname for the 10th Duke used by his friends) had told me that this was a very important day for him as it was the hundredth anniversary of his father's birthday – a father of whom he was very fond and who was also a great fox-hunter and sportsman.

'On the opposite bank of the river was a wood in which there was a litter of fox cubs and, on this particular summer day, one of the brood bitches from the kennels decided to leave her whelps for a short time and give the vixen a bit of exercise. Just as Master hooked his first fish of the day, he heard the old bitch "open" (that is, of hounds, to give tongue when they get the scent) and, looking up, saw the fox, closely followed by the foxhound, pass by along the opposite bank. He cheered her on and a few minutes later landed his fish.'

Sir Peter's son, Captain Ian Farquhar, MVO, MFH, became Joint Master of the Beaufort in 1985. We talked in the library of the house he lives in on the estate at Badminton, surrounded by sporting books and any number of elegant hunting pictures. Here you will find not only Beckford and Surtees on the shelves but the stud books giving the pedigrees of hounds stretching back two hundred years; those hounds which he and his father have spent so much of their time perfecting.

He explained that there were two main ways of running a hunt. Under the old system 'the mastership takes a guarantee from the country [that is to say, from the area within which the hunt operates]. Let us say the country can raise ten or twenty or thirty or a hundred thousand pounds a year and that will be passed on to you and you then run the country to the best of your ability. It is not usually quite enough, and the master has to top it up from his own pocket.

'In quite a lot of hunts now people are short of cash and don't take an open-ended agreement. Instead, you often get a joint mastership making a one-year contract from 1 May to 1 May for a set amount. Whichever way you choose, all hunts are now run under the rules of the Master of Foxhounds Association, and must be registered with it.'

What makes a good master? 'A great deal of organization goes into it. You've got to be a diplomat and a politician. You've got to get to know everybody. There are six or seven hundred bona fide farmers in a country like this, and three or four hundred smaller landowners with, say, thirty or forty acres you are liable to go across. Literally ninety-nine per cent are agreeable, and very many farmers hunt with us; it's a very, very strong tradition here. The farming community are the backbone of hunting.'

How would a beginner go about joining a celebrated hunt like the Beaufort? 'The membership is open to anyone who farms here as a right; and up to recently anyone who *lives* within the hunt; twenty or thirty years ago you could just apply to the secretary and hunt in whatever country you liked. Now it's much more limited to hunting in your own country, so the number of people from outside is very limited too.' So if a complete stranger does arrange a day's hunting, does he have to conform to the rules? 'Obviously there's an understood pattern of behaviour. Over the years a country code has evolved which takes into account different farming patterns, and discipline is maintained by the Masters and Field Masters, bearing in mind at all times that the hunt are guests of those who farm the land.'

What would a good day's hunting involve? 'It's much more complex than it at first appears to get a satisfactory day's sport. First, you must be welcome on the land, and able to cross the land you propose to hunt. That means warning cards must be sent out to people whose land you may cross. Then the coverts

The blue and buff of the Beaufort Hunt – one of the smartest
in the country.

*Above: All part of the fun – the Wessex Yeomanry race before the
hunt begins.
Previous page: The Vale of the White Horse in line abreast –
all shapes, ages, and sizes.*

must be accessible, and attractive to the quarry, which of course has the spin-off of being equally attractive to all forms of wild life, so it in itself promotes conservation. For example, many hedgerows and woods would be gone if it were not for hunting. Hounds, horses and staff have to be organized, and then you have people like the terrier men and the fence menders who are an essential back-up to the day's sport.'

The Beaufort has two joint Masters (the present, 11th Duke of Beaufort and Ian Farquhar), a hunt secretary and a field secretary: 'The secretaries run the books and the warning cards, and help with the public relations work both with the farming community and the world at large. Then you have the kennel huntsman, the first and second whippers-in, and three others looking after hounds and collecting flesh from the farms.' The collection of flesh – an arcane activity to the non-hunter – is a service offered by the hunt to farmers: 'In return for the hunt clearing the countryside of fallen stock the farmers help with the massive task of feeding 120 large hounds. For instance, it takes a large cow or fifteen good calves a day to feed a pack of hounds.'

Essential to the sport is a pack of hounds that hunts well. Hundreds of generations of hounds have been bred for hunting alone since 1770: 'I can't think of another animal to compare with it for breeding.' What he looks for is 'shoulders, feet, constitution, determination, perseverance, nose, voice, and fox sense; you want to produce a pack who will hunt under difficult conditions.' And what about the elusive question of scent? 'There are no rules. Generally speaking you want the ground warmer than the air and a steady glass; and a moist westerly wind is better than an easterly; but conditions that are good in October can often be useless in March. A vixen gives off less scent than a dog-fox in the spring.' And what about the kill? How often does it happen? 'A four-day-a-week hunt kills eighty or ninety brace a year. The majority of people who go out hunting don't even know when it happens. For the followers the act of killing is of little consequence. The compulsion is that whatever happens you keep up with that pack of hounds. You take falls and break bones. Fear gets the adrenalin going, and the cry of a pack of hounds running hard can often be spellbinding; this unison of man, horse and hounds working in accord is totally compelling. It's hard to explain to someone who's not done it.'

Someone who most assuredly has done it is Martin Scott, till last year Master of the Vale of the White Horse and an old friend of Ian Farquhar's and scion of a notable sporting family: his grandfather, Mason Thompson Scott, and his great uncle both played rugby for England; his father was a Master of Foxhounds with only one four-year gap from 1927 to 1965. He first went hunting in a basket at the age of two: 'One didn't *know* one's parents particularly well, but one did know one's grooms.' He served three years in a cavalry regiment, the Royal Dragoons, taking his annual six-week hunting leave every November. In 1969, at the tender age of twenty-four, he became joint Master of the Tiverton Hounds with Lady Amory. 'I lived in a cottage rent free. I had to do all the hound work. I was up at seven every morning, cleaned the kennels, exercised the hounds, and went out collecting dead animals.' Then after eight years at Tiverton (a two-day-a-week hunt) he moved to the VWH: 'It's a much better country to cross and it's a four-day-a-week hunt.' When he finally gave up last year it was to earn some money (though he now hunts with the Beaufort). 'I had fifteen years as a Master when I was young, fit and healthy.'

He too felt the relationship with the farmers was central to the success of the hunt. 'Even though you are wet and tired, you must go back the same night and tell the farmers before they know if something's gone wrong and cattle may have got out. We take stakes in the van with us and, as a rule, anything broken by the hunt is repaired by the hunt.' A hunt fencer would be out mending fences next day, sometimes with the farmer's help. Yet he freely admitted there was a dichotomy between the criteria of a good hunt and the continuing allegiance of the farmers: 'The object of the exercise is to provide the field with as much heartache and thrill as possible while doing as little damage as possible; but you must be prepared to repair the damage.'

His list of the qualities that made a good Master tallied with Ian Farquhar's, though he added one more: 'He must be able to drink a lot but never get drunk.' The skills have not changed, he thought, since Beckford's time: 'The huntsman's job is to get the hounds to keep together. You put the hounds into a covert and then some of them open and speak. We can smell a fox, boys, they say, come and join us. They hunt by noses, not by sight, ninety-nine per cent of the time. The cry of the hounds in woodlands is a lovely noise; then it changes as they come out into the open. Now the huntsman's job is to get the hounds away together as pack; then to think what will make the hounds check; for example, he must know where the wind is all the time, and perhaps look ahead to anticipate what is likely to cause a check.'

And what would it all cost nowadays? 'This depends entirely on your situation. For the farmer, looking after and breeding his own horses, the cost will be considerably less than for someone like myself who is hunting as a subscriber. First you've got to buy a horse. For someone of my size (heavy-weight) that would be £3,000 to £4,000. Then you have to keep it. It will cost you £55 a week to keep in livery; much less if you do it yourself (though it's as well not to add it up or it might put you off doing it). A set of shoes, for instance, costs £15 and lasts a month. Then if you're more than six miles from the meet you'll need some transport; a trailer or lorry. The subscription for a four-day-a-week here (in VWH country) is £600 a year; in other parts of the country where the hunting's not so fashion-able it would cost you only about £200 a year. In the majority of England farmers hunt for much less in return for providing the land. But one of the great pleasures of hunting is that it takes you to places you would never normally see. I've been recently to places like Sodbury Common and West Littleton, beautiful places you just don't see from a car; places I didn't know existed.'

Both Ian and Martin agreed that hunting involves people from every imaginable walk of life: peers and publicans, doctors and dentists, lawyers and labourers, ministers and miners. 'In Wales,' said Martin, 'there's a miners' pack; and when I was in Devon we had a postman who used to hunt; on those occasions people received their mail either very early or very late.'

So what was the point of it all? 'Finding a fox, galloping as far and fast as possible after it and catching it. It's seeing hounds hunt the fox; hearing the cry of the hounds. It needs a little bit of wisdom and a little bit of madness.'

Where

The Shires of England are renowned the world over in hunting circles for housing most of the well-known packs of foxhounds. The three most 'fashionable' packs are considered to be the Quorn (Leicestershire, Derbyshire and Nottingham-shire); the Belvoir (Leicestershire and Lincolnshire); and the Beaufort (Gloucester-shire, Avon and Wiltshire). Visitors wishing to ride with a particular hunt should contact the secretary. Descriptions of packs and details of the secretary and other staff can be found in Baily's Hunting Directory (available at £18 from J.A. Allen & Co. Ltd, 1 Lower Grosvenor Place, London SW1W OEL). Other information about the sport can be obtained from The British Field Sports Society, 59 Kennington Road, London SE1 7PZ (tel. 01 928 4742).

When

Usually the opening meet of a hunt takes place on the Saturday nearest 1 November, and hounds generally meet at 11 a.m. From that day onwards a full subscription or 'cap' is expected and visitors are required to introduce themselves to the Master and to pay their cap and field money. Fixture details can be found in Horse and Hound *magazine, which is published every Friday (address: King's Reach Tower, Stamford Street, London SE1 9LS).*

NEW YEAR'S EVE

DECEMBER

'And Christmas-morning bells say "Come!" / Even to shining ones who dwell / Safe in the Dorchester Hotel,' as John Betjeman reminds us; and not only in the Dorchester but in the Ritz and indeed every major London hotel. The Ritz offered thirteen days of junketing which opened with dinner and cabaret on Friday 20 December 1985 and continued with carols in the Long Gallery on the following four nights from six to seven; champagne and traditional Christmas lunch on the 25th for a mere £48.75; a tea dance on Boxing Day for a mere £15; and then, on New Year's Eve, a gala dinner dance with four-course menu and dancing to The Runcible Spoon till two for a nicely judged £95 each. Service and tax were included, as well they might be; but by the time they'd ordered a bottle of Grande Dame champagne and a couple of apéritifs, no couple would escape at much under £250. Was there therefore some hesitation before the room filled up? Not a bit of it; every one of the 142 seats in the Ritz's Restaurant – arguably the most beautiful in Europe – was taken weeks before.

Contrary to the received idea, the Ritz is not over-whelmed by Americans or even Australians, Germans or Japanese. Most of its clients remain English; though not all the Englishmen who foregather there were born on the right side of the tracks. One regular, for example, is a scrap metal merchant who made his first killing out of a skip parked right outside the plush hostelry and who comes each New Year on a sentimental journey to celebrate his good fortune. The music is pretty middle of the road ('Strangers in the Night') but the piper at midnight provides a proper Gaelic, or shall we say Hogmanay, overtone; and in an inspired move, Julian Payne, manager of the Ritz, has introduced the idea of fireworks as the New Year is ushered in; a barrage of fizzing catherine wheels and vaunting rockets on the balcony just outside the great windows that protect Ritz customers from the vulgar or at any rate poorer world without. The sight of so many ritzy people pressing their faces like children to the Ritz windows to see the kaleidoscopic fun is something I shall not easily forget; nor shall I quickly erase the image of the young cadre of Italian and French waiters kissing all the waitresses, impervious for the nonce of their duties, as the clock struck midnight. In those turbulent few minutes, the whole of the Ritz seemed to lose its

There were angels dining at the Ritz – or so the old song says

Here's looking at you kid: New Year strikes at the Ritz.

sense of place and form and to dissolve into a Dionysiac rave-up, the served and the servers blending together riotously in the knees-up. Then order was restored – of a kind; for the raunchy American singer Bertice Reading came on to sock it to the revellers for a further hour; and then there was more dancing, with only one small fire caused by some streamers catching in the candles, happily quickly doused, to create any untoward excitement. Carriages were at two, and the Ritz goers seemed pleased enough with their evening; while the Ritz management shared their pleasure, being some £20,000 the richer.

How to get in

Most major London hotels arrange special celebrations for New Year's Eve. Last year, as we have seen, the Ritz Hotel charged £95 per person for their bash, which included dinner, dancing, and a firework display, but not drinks. The party lasts from 8 p.m. to 2 a.m. and the dress is black tie. The hotel also has a special rate for New Year's Eve accommodation of £70 per person for one night, inclusive of breakfast, service charge and VAT. Reservations for the party can be made by contacting: The Restaurant Manager, Ritz Hotel, Piccadilly, London W1V 9 DG (tel.01 493 8181).

How to get there

The Ritz is in Piccadilly in the heart of London's West End. Although the hotel is next to Green Park Underground Station it would be wiser to avoid travelling on the Tube late at night in formal wear. Car parking spaces near the hotel are very limited, and a taxi is by far the best method of arriving and departing.

MEDITATION THE MORNING AFTER

Anyone who follows the modern English season right through its year-long span has every right now to sit back and relax. We have seen the English at play from the solstice to the equinox and back: what lessons, if any, can we learn from the punishing experience?

There is first the charge against the season itself that it is not what it was. Yet nor is any other English institution. The decline of Ascot, as we have seen, has been noted and deplored for at least a century. Any bounder can hire himself a morning coat at Moss Bros; no doubt many have done so. Money and know-how (and perhaps we should add time) will buy you into just about any of the great social events in the English calendar; unless, that is, you are a world-famous gaolbird or *mafioso*; and even then money and *chutzpah* have been known to work the trick. The fact is that money has oiled the wheels of sport for centuries now; indeed they would not turn without it.

Does money, then, *ruin* sport? To read some of the most celebrated commentators of English society you would be sure that it did. We have discussed Nigel Dempster's blistering attack on the commercialism of Royal Ascot; but he is not alone in his strictures. The *Tatler*, still England's most influential chronicler of high society, recently ran a well-documented tirade against the inexorable rise of business in the English social season. In a wincingly snobbish piece Vicki Woods portrayed the upper-class wife of a company chairman aghast at the sort of people she now had to mix with. 'The day is long past when her husband, now the company chairman, watched his races in his father's box, or Camilla's stepfather's box or indeed his own box. This box is now the company's box and this elegant woman has to share the champagne, strawberries and the silent cricket scores with a northern area sales manager and his boring bloody wife in her cheap hat and tight apricot suit you can see her knickers through which looks as though it would be more at home in Tenerife on the back of a football manager's mistress. Who are all these people?' She provides her own answer.

They are people who have been invited by big business. 'These people at the Derby, at Ascot, at Wimbledon, at Henley, at Glorious Goodwood are standing in boxes that their companies have hired. For the day, for the week, for the whole glorious social fortnight. It is a fabulous place to see clients, a wonderful place to do deals, a great place to show off in. Crown Wallpaper is here, IBM is here, Plessey is here, the banks, the building societies, Shell UK, Burmah Castrol, Courage Breweries, Thames TV, *Daily Mirror*, the big builders, the big advertising agencies, the butchers, the bakers and the Lymeswold cheese makers.'

One by one, she claims, the bastions have fallen; culminating that year with Ever Ready's deal at Epsom. For the first time Epsom owners, United Racecourses, bowed to sponsorship of the whole caboodle, accepting a three-year deal from Ever Ready Batteries worth £1.8 million. This sum provided the much-needed finance to restore the weathered wedding cake of Epsom facilities. The result was that anyone who was a guest of Ever Ready had a grandstand view of the racing and could mingle with such nobs as Mrs Michael Caine, Evelyn de Rothschild and Woodrow Wyatt.

The thesis was developed by Stephen Aris in *The Sunday Times* Magazine during the summer of 1986. All that remains, he claims, of what used to be called The Season is a series of grand formal occasions concentrated in a few glorious weeks – Wimbledon, Henley, Ascot, Glyndebourne – which are more popular than ever. 'And who goes to them? The answer, to the distress of those professional snobs, the society columnists, is all sorts: socialites and social climbers, captains of industry and DIY millionaires, advertising men and media folk and, if the corporate hosts are to be believed, plane-loads of their foreign, tax-deductible clients.'

At Wimbledon, he asserts, there are forty-four commercial tents in the All England Club's grounds, bringing in upwards of £5,000 a day each. Midland Bank is just one Company who take it very seriously; they charter planes to fly in their French and German clients from Lyons and Düsseldorf. In 1985, Wimbledon made a profit of just over £5 million on a turnover of £12.75 million – including £8.1 million from world-wide television rights, £2.2 million from tickets sales, £2.1 million from promotion and marketing. At Henley, there are at least five tented villages on the *rive gauche* (the Berkshire side) where firms can entertain guests to lunch, courtesy of veteran caterers Payne and Gunter, for £100 a head.

Money, he claims, talks at Glyndebourne too: 'The main reason why tickets ... are so hard to come by is that the majority, some eighty-five per cent, are reserved for the five thousand individual Friends of Glyndebourne (the list has been closed for years) and for the 225 corporate members who pay £1,500-£2,000 a year for an allotment of up to 136 tickets a year. Those tickets which are not taken up (bankers prefer Mozart and Verdi to Stravinsky and Janàcek) tend to be sold out within a matter of hours.'

Aris sums up: 'The Season may not be quite what it was; but the attraction remains as potent as ever. It's quite a trick to pull people in their thousands and yet maintain the pretence that these events are the preserve of a privileged few. The Real Old Smart are smarter than you think.'

But what is so new about all this? Money has always been mixed with sport, and society has always been renewed by injections of money from big business. In 1894 the Russian Czarevitch wrote home to his mother, the Empress Marie, complaining that the members of the party given by the Prince of Wales (later Edward VII) were mostly horse dealers. But there was worse to come. By the turn of the century Edward's intimate friends included the millionaire grocer, Sir Thomas Lipton, who poured a fortune into big yacht racing, and the furniture manufacturer, Sir Blundell Maple, who spent so much money on horses that, to his intense pleasure, he was elected to the super-exclusive Jockey Club in 1903. As Sir Philip Magnus remarked of him in his *Life of Edward VII*, 'He understood perfectly the undertones governing the relationship between the pre-revolutionary aristocracy of land and birth, and representatives of the fallen Imperial régime who were associated with banking and commerce.'

Perhaps what these castigators of modern society are really complaining about is not so much money as new money. Thus the *Tatler* piece went on to differentiate between the mixture of Real Old Smart and Brash New Commerce at Henley Royal Regatta. The OK people were on the right hand side of the river in the Stewards' Enclosure and Leander Club, while 'all the hundreds and hundreds of northern area sales managers are neatly contained on the *rive gauche*'. What the Tatler did not explain, in this subtle social analysis, was that the President of Henley is a man called John Garton, Eton, Oxford, and the Scots Guards, and obviously therefore, as anyone meeting him will at once know, a *chevalier sans peur et sans reproche*. But the family fortunes derive from his ancestor, a Victorian grocer called Garton who invented HP sauce. Some time in the last hundred years his family has crossed the river.

Ah no, return the Stylites of modern society, it isn't the money we complain of; it's the snobbery; the sense of one-upmanship all these events convey. Simon Barnes of *The Times* put it eloquently after the 1986 Henley. 'The sport,' he asserted, 'is secondary – no, tertiary at best. What is primary is the wearing of the right badge .... For the Great Game that is being played at these events is the Grand Royal and Ancient Sport of Snobbery. At all events there is a graded range of enclosure. The most important people at the event are not the sportsmen, but the gatemen, whose duty and obvious pleasure it is to exclude people who have the Wrong Badge.'

Obviously there are people who feel like this; Simon Barnes himself for a start. Yet if that is what the real pleasure is about, it is an ephemeral and illusory one. Having the right badge to the Stewards' Enclosure at Henley, for instance, is merely a passport to a long, hot, weary queue for lunch in one of the marquees. The really smart Henley punters are the ones who've tied up their rowing boat outside the boom for nothing or are picnicking on the grass beside their car. Of course you could have a People's Henley in which there were no tickets at all; but I fear the Stylites of this world would soon clamour for punitive action by central government to end the chaos that would surely result.

There are any number of theses to be written about the season; any number of dashing theories to be constructed. We hinted at the beginning of this book that, for example, one elegant definition of the season might be all those events where Veuve Clicquot champagne is on sale. It would be a fine list; and might well demonstrate graphically the rise of champagne in our country's fortunes, in flat contradiction of all the other depressing indices. The British import more champagne from France than any other race in the world; more than the United States, more than Germany, more than Japan. In 1985 we imported 15,351,080 bottles – a million more than the

Americans, nearly twice as many as the Germans. Not only does bubbly slake the thirsts of thousands of *aficionados* at every great English sporting occasion; it actually helps turn the wheels of many key events. Mumm champagne, as we have seen, back the Admiral's Cup at Cowes week; Lanson have a race named after them at Goodwood; Laurent/Perrier help pay for Polo, and so do Taittinger; Perrier-Jouet finance the Oaks at Epsom: and Veuve Clicquot initiated the idea of champagne on the lawns of Wimbledon.

It depends where you stand politically and socially when you come to decide whether all this conspicuous consumption is a good thing. Champagne has become a vastly more popular drink since the last world war. No footballer worth his salt celebrates a big win with anything less nowadays. Giant bottles of Moët et Chandon stand ready to be shaken with appalling vigour at the end of many a motor race; the connexion is so close that the former world champion driver Jackie Stewart is now a director of the celebrated *marque*. Champagne is a drink with many obvious advantages. The ceremony of opening and pouring it is euphoric; the bubbles quickly induce a mood of well-being, yet it is far less likely to trouble the breathalyser than whisky or gin. It is a unisex drink. It can be drunk all round the clock and with any sort of food or with no food at all. It goes splendidly with picnics; and it's no coincidence that the great champagne house of Krug has initiated two picnic contests at Henley, one for professional cooks, one for amateurs.

We could develop another doctoral thesis on the picnic – that enduring monument to the English genius for improvisation and talent for ignoring some of the most inhospitable weather in the civilized world. We could trace the picnic from its homely beginnings, from the cold meat, tea, bread, butter and jam taken up the Thames by the *Three Men in a Boat* to the elaborate refections of today. We could contrast the handy potted shrimps and sloe gin of the shooting fraternity with the barbecues and plonk of the rugby fans; the friendly spread on the lawn at Lord's with the ornate charade behind the ha-ha at Glyndebourne; we could chart the spread of booze from the Pimm's at Henley to the bubbly at Ascot; and we could no doubt with patience deduce just about all we needed to know about the nature of the season by a minute study of the prevalence of

smoked salmon – just as the palaeontologists can reconstruct a dinosaur from a bone in its toe. But that really would need another whole book on its own.

Manifestly there will be those who purse their lips at all this jollity; we still divide naturally into puritans and cavaliers. There will be those who see the season as no more than the ostentation of wealth and the flaunting of privilege. There will be those who retort that you can still see the Derby or tie your boat at Henley for nothing. There is some truth in both views.

Certain events in the season – the blood sports – face not simply moral charges but also the lively threat of political action. The Beaufort Hunt, with whom I spent some time in writing this book, say they generally have to reckon with an anti-hunt demonstration only two or three times in their six-month season, though these receive a disproportionate amount of publicity. Much more worrying to the fox hunting world is the prospect of a Labour government pledged to abolish their sport. I spent some time talking informally to Ian Farquhar and Martin Scott about this, and found them reasonably certain that fox hunting would be banned in their lifetimes. Ireland seemed the best bet if it happened; for hunting is something neither of them could happily live without. They admitted to being on the defensive about hunting; the only answer they could see would be to go into the great industrial cities and try to educate the town dwellers in what they see as the naturalness and inevitability of hunting. It would cost a lot of money, and who would do it? 'Not blimps like us.'

For myself, I take a neutral stance on the moral issue. I have no desire to hunt, but have no objection to others hunting provided they do not abrogate to themselves rights other sports do not enjoy. Nature is red in tooth and claw; the fields and woods are full of predators; *homo sapiens* is just one of them. No one who lives in the country and has seen what a fox can do to a chicken-run during the night will have all that much sympathy with him; whether foxes would flourish at all if there were no fox hunting is a nice point. Since I began this book I have come to understand much more clearly the subtleties and complexities of hunting and can imagine it might be an agreeable way to spend a Saturday in the autumn; how people can want to hunt four times a week defeats me still. The grand old Duke of Beaufort, who spent more time out hunting than any man alive, was called with some justice the most pointless man in England.

After a good day's shooting, my kind host Norman MacRoberts remarked, you sleep well. I'm sure you do: but perhaps it depends on your not having to worry about your public persona as the Royals do. It's a good rule for all pheasant to avoid Sandringham, where each Prince of Wales in turn has vied with his predecessor over who can shoot the most. 'I love shooting more than anything else,' the future Edward VIII wrote to his father, George V, in 1912. In later life he could still remember the best days: 'A good day's bag was a thousand head; but two thousand was not unknown on the large estates.' There were days, however, when even George V said, 'Perhaps we went a little too far today, David.'

A little? On 18 December 1913 at the Beaconsfield estate of Lord Burnham all royal records were broken. The Duke of Windsor (as he eventually became) recalled: 'My left arm ached from lifting my gun, and I was deaf and stunned from the banging …. When, in the late afternoon, the carnage stopped, almost four thousand pheasant had been killed. The bright limp carcasses were laid out in rows of a hundred; the whole place was littered with feathers and spent cartridges. My father had shot over a thousand birds. He was proud of the way he had shot that day, but I think that the scale of the bag troubled even his conscience.' And these days, indeed, a good bag would be measured in hundreds rather than thousands. It is a sport which has fascinated men for hundreds of years, but also repelled them. In a haunting passage written two hundred years ago, Alexander Pope described how: 'Whirring pheasant springs / And mounts exulting on triumphant wings: / Short is his joy; he feels the fiery wound / Flutters in blood, and panting beats the ground.'

It is a scene that has not varied in the two centuries since he wrote that. The beauty of the pheasant is perfectly captured by such an expert shot as Anthony Burghersh in *The Debrett Season*: 'Pheasant climb and accelerate with great ease for a large bird and once airborne are electric with colour and grace …. The guns raise their weapons with a well-practised swing and unleash a hail of lead into the sky. A fine cock bird, its head thrown back, its wings collapsed, begins its slow spiral to the hard ground.'

It does not seem to me that the odds for the pheasant are all that sporting. Few get away from an organized shoot like the one I witnessed. As Pope summed up – 'Ah! What avail his glossy, varying dyes / His purple crest and scarlet-circled eyes / The vivid green his shining plumes unfold / His painted wings and breast that flames with gold?' What indeed.

Fishing gets by far the least flak of the three major blood sports (and which Labour government will be bold enough to outlaw this favoured pursuit of the toiling millions?). John Birth put it to me that while in hunting and shooting there is not much left at the end of the day's sport of either fox or pheasant, the trout has a sporting chance of being returned to the water to be fished another day. I am not sure I should enjoy the experience of being that trout. Byron has a celebrated stanza in *Don Juan*: 'And angling, too, that solitary vice / Whatever Izaak Walton sings or says / The quaint old cruel coxcomb, in his gullet / Should have a hook, and a small trout to pull it.' He added in a note that fishing to him was 'the cruellest, the coldest, and the stupidest of pretended sports.' It should be freely admitted that his is a distinctly minority view; and the literature celebrating the mystique and mesmeric fascination of fishing is immense. Over this sport, as over the others, I do not propose to take sides; except perhaps to say that in each it is the pleasure of the chase which seems to matter even more than the kill; if there is cruelty, it is incidental, not an end in itself.

There is one last point about the English season. It is unique. No other country in the world can offer such a cornucopia of diversions in one continuous cycle and in such small space. All of them can be enjoyed within an easy drive of London. The last convulsion of a spent empire, or the urbane mode of a ripe civilization? I do not propose to take sides on this issue either: decide for yourselves. The English season is what you make of it, like so much else in English life. There is one issue, however, on which I will take any odds you like: the English season is here to stay.

BREAD AND BUTTER LETTER

My first thanks once again go to Colin Webb, managing director of Pavilion Books. *The English Season* was entirely his idea, and he has followed the progress of his brainchild with a heartening parental care. Few publishers nowadays have his enviable gift for conjuring obviously good ideas from thin air, to which the vigorous growth of his fledgling firm in its first few years is the best testimony.

I must next thank Homer Sykes for proving such a lively and steadfast partner. Most photographers, in my experience, live on their nerves and show it. Homer is as avid for the perfect shot as the next man; but through all our adventures never lost his sense of humour. He ran many miles in pursuit of his hunting pictures, for example, while I followed at a more sedate pace; but his energy clearly paid. He was a pleasure to work with.

I am indeed grateful to Adam Helliker for lending his expert help. As I explain in the list of books consulted, his *Debrett Season* is the last attempt to look at the whole subject. I have not only drawn on it freely, but also had the benefit of his help over the 'How To' sections which end each chapter. In addition, he has proved a trusted adviser throughout, and has read the manuscript twice, making many valuable suggestions. He should not, however, be held responsible for any blemishes which remain.

Oscar Turnill has again brought not only his formidable editing skills but also his wide knowledge of many sports discussed to bear on my text; while at Pavilion Books, Sue Mitchell has handled the manuscript with tact and care. I am also greatly indebted to Steve Dobell there for pointing out many lacunae in early drafts, and for getting the book to press with such professional dispatch. Once again I must thank Judith Woolliams, who cheerfully typed the many drafts, and my daughter Amanda Smith, who researched with her customary zing.

I must now thank my good friends and neighbours Lord and Lady Oaksey for their unfailing patience and kindness. They are, I think, enviably unusual in the span of their horizons. Nobody knows more about horses then they do; and though both have had serious riding mishaps, they have pursued other interests with undiminished vim, John broadcasting and writing,

Tory painting and exhibiting at the Royal Academy Summer Show. I could not possibly have had such an entrée to the equestrian world without their generous help, and I have dedicated the book to them as a small token of my thanks.

So many people helped me with individual events that it is impossible to thank them all; but I am particularly grateful to the following: Air Commodore Robert Weighill, then secretary of the Rugby Football Union, gave me a most helpful briefing on the logistics of Twickenham; Mr Chris Dodd, rowing correspondent of *The Guardian*, befriended me as a tyro in the Boat Race press boat and generously advised me both on that and Henley Royal Regatta; and through the good offices of Mr Dan Topolski I was able to dine with the Oxford crew shortly before the 1986 race and so get a first-hand experience of that fascinating world. I am under a special debt to Mr John Garton, President of Henley Royal Regatta, and to his wife, for the remarkable insights into that most English of summer diversions, drawn on an intimate knowledge gained over half a century, that they were kind enough to give me.

At the Royal Academy I was fortunate enough to have long talks to three key figures: the President, Mr Roger de Grey; his immediate predecessor, Sir Hugh Casson; and that treasury of Academy lore, Mr Sidney Hutchison. Miss Fiona Sacher kindly arranged, moreover, for me to be at the private view.

In the same way Miss Valerie Hart was good enough to arrange for me to be at the private view of the Chelsea Flower Show; and here too I was given generous help by my colleague Graham Rose, gardening correspondent of *The Sunday Times*.

My debt to that archetypal fisherman Mr John Birth will be clear to all who read the chapter on trout fishing; I am grateful equally to Mr Norman MacRoberts for so kindly allowing me to join his pheasant shooting party and to his friends who also gave me unstinted insights into their sport; and my obligation to Captain Ian Farquhar, joint Master of the Beaufort Hunt, and his friend Mr Martin Scott, former Master of the Vale of the White Horse Hunt, will be immediately plain. Mr Jim Gilmore not only provided useful background information about the Beaufort but also was unendingly helpful over Badminton.

I was fortunate enough to be the guest of Lady Grade at the Rose Ball, while Mr Magnus Linklater, an Etonian himself and father of an Eton boy, was good enough to take me with him to the Fourth of June celebrations. Mr Peter Lawrence, an authority on Eton, gave me the benefit of his great wisdom on its history. Mr Michael Shea kindly arranged for me to be a guest at a Buckingham Palace Garden Party; and Major R.A. Courage helpfully arranged for me to see for myself the inner workings of Trooping the Colour at one of the dress rehearsals.

I was able to call on the formidable expertise of friends in two key summer events: Mr Maurice Graham, himself formerly a keen polo player and father of two excellent present-day players, gave me invaluable background on the sport; while Mr Graeme Jenkins, the gifted young conductor of the Glyndebourne Touring Company, was able to take me behind the scenes there, and give me most useful inside knowledge of the company's work.

Mr Stuart Alexander proved a charming and knowledgeable guide at Cowes, as befits an England yachtsman, while Mr Robin Marlar was an equally valuable authority on the lore of Lord's. My old friend Mr Nicholas Mason was good enough to check the cricket text for accuracy and to provide a number of helpful suggestions.

I was the guest of that resourceful entrepreneur Mr Roy Ackerman at the Last Night of the Proms, and also at the Henley Festival which now follows directly after the Regatta and was his happy inspiration; while Mr Julian Payne, manager of the Ritz, proved a most agreeable host at the New Year's Eve celebrations there.

Mr Michael Coley was my kind host at Hurlingham and Mr Brian Macmillan, administrative secretary of the Croquet Association, guided my faltering footsteps into that most arcane of English sports.

Two ladies who came most opportunely to my aid were Miss Joanne Dillon of United Racecourses, who went to much trouble to consult Derby records for me; and Ms Paula MacMillan, of the All England Lawn Tennis and Croquet Club, who saved my chapter on Wimbledon from a number of mistakes.

I was struck in preparing this book with the pervasive role of champagne in the season and was lucky enough to be able to consult a number of knowledgeable people on the point. Mr Malcolm McIntyre of the Champagne Bureau supplied copious statistics, and no fewer than four of the leading importers of celebrated marques were generous enough to talk to me and to entertain me most hospitably at the same time: Anthony Leschallas (Bollinger); David Hodges (Krug); Michael Druitt (Perrier-Jouet); and John Clevely (Veuve Clicquot).

Godfrey Smith

INDEX

Here's to the next season of top hats, tails and traditions…